Pro jQuery in Oracle Application Express

Scott Wesley

⟨IOUG⟩
independent oracle users group

Apress®

Pro jQuery in Oracle Application Express

ISBN-13 (pbk): 978-1-4842-0962-2

ISBN-13 (electronic): 978-1-4842-0961-5

Managing Director: Welmoed Spahr
Lead Editor: Jonathan Gennick
Technical Reviewer: Alex Fatkulin
Editorial Board: Steve Anglin, Louise Corrigan, Jim DeWolf, Jonathan Gennick, Robert Hutchinson, Michelle Lowman, James Markham, Susan McDermott, Matthew Moodie, Jeffrey Pepper, Douglas Pundick, Ben Renow-Clarke, Gwenan Spearing
Coordinating Editor: Jill Balzano
Copy Editor: Ann Dickson
Compositor: SPi Global
Indexer: SPi Global
Artist: SPi Global
Cover Designer: Anna Ishchenko

Distributed to the book trade worldwide by Springer Science+Business Media New York, 233 Spring Street, 6th Floor, New York, NY 10013. Phone 1-800-SPRINGER, fax (201) 348-4505, e-mail orders-ny@springer-sbm.com, or visit www.springer.com. Apress Media, LLC is a California LLC and the sole member (owner) is Springer Science + Business Media Finance Inc (SSBM Finance Inc). SSBM Finance Inc is a Delaware corporation.

For information on translations, please e-mail rights@apress.com, or visit www.apress.com.

Apress and friends of ED books may be purchased in bulk for academic, corporate, or promotional use. eBook versions and licenses are also available for most titles. For more information, reference our Special Bulk Sales–eBook Licensing web page at www.apress.com/bulk-sales.

Any source code or other supplementary material referenced by the author in this text is available to readers at www.apress.com. For detailed information about how to locate your book's source code, go to www.apress.com/source-code/.

I would like to thank all the scientists and visionaries that make modern life possible.

About IOUG Press

IOUG Press is a joint effort by the **Independent Oracle Users Group (the IOUG)** *and* **Apress** *to deliver some of the highest-quality content possible on Oracle Database and related topics. The IOUG is the world's leading, independent organization for professional users of Oracle products. Apress is a leading, independent technical publisher known for developing high-quality, no-fluff content for serious technology professionals. The IOUG and Apress have joined forces in IOUG Press to provide the best content and publishing opportunities to working professionals who use Oracle products.*

Our shared goals include:

- Developing content with excellence
- Helping working professionals to succeed
- Providing authoring and reviewing opportunities
- Networking and raising the profiles of authors and readers

To learn more about Apress, visit our website at **www.apress.com**. Follow the link for IOUG Press to see the great content that is now available on a wide range of topics that matter to those in Oracle's technology sphere.

Visit **www.ioug.org** to learn more about the Independent Oracle Users Group and its mission. Consider joining if you haven't already. Review the many benefits at www.ioug.org/join. Become a member. Get involved with peers. Boost your career.

www.ioug.org/join

Apress®

Contents at a Glance

Contents

About the Author

Scott Wesley has been working with Oracle development tools since finishing a computer science degree in 2000. Since then Scott has actively researched and applied cutting-edge technologies from the Oracle product range in projects spanning retail, government, finance, and construction sectors.

Based in Perth, Australia, Scott started on Oracle 8.1.7 with Oracle Forms and Reports 6i, dabbled with mod_plsql, and now designs and develops data-centric web applications using the Oracle APEX technology stack. In addition to his consulting duties with SAGE Computing Services, he also enjoys meeting and teaching students about APEX, PL/SQL, and SQL. In 2014 he was recognized as an Oracle ACE.

Scott has been a regular presenter at Australian user-group events since 2007. Aided with the fresh "prezi" delivery style, his passion for presenting earned him Best Paper in 2011 for his presentation "APEX 4.1 Security." In 2013 he published a video series titled "Oracle APEX Techniques" and finally experienced his first Kscope in 2015, presenting an APEX best practices session and a popular deep dive on jQuery.

Scott combats geographic isolation by contributing to the community through various online avenues such as his blog at grassroots-oracle.com. You'll also find him on the OTN forums, Twitter @swesley_perth, and more recently in the #orclapex channels at Slack. Given the chance, he will talk your ear off with enthusiasm about science and skepticism, preferably while playing pool or eating a hot curry.

About the Technical Reviewer

Alex Fatkulin is a master of the full range of Oracle technologies. His mastery has been essential in addressing some of the greatest challenges his customers have met.

Alex draws on years of experience working with some of the world's largest companies, where he has been involved with almost everything related to Oracle databases, from data modeling to architecting high-availability solutions to resolving performance issues of extremely large production sites.

Alex has a bachelor's of computer science degree from Far Eastern National University in Vladivostok, Russia. He is also an Oracle ACE and a proud OakTable member.

Acknowledgments

I'd first like to acknowledge the broader development community—from my colleagues on software projects, to bloggers I read, people I teach, delegates I meet at conferences, and technologists I interact with on forums. We stand with some giants, and without this collaboration we wouldn't be working with such a great development tool today. I would like to encourage everyone to start with a small step toward getting more involved in the Oracle community.

More specifically, I would like to thank Connor McDonald. Living in the same small city, we have crossed paths on a few projects. While learning from the effective creativity that is his brain, I was also able to find my path in my own career.

This path helped me end up working for Penny Cookson. She has generously provided me with the support I need to learn, explore, share, and grow my career, all the while treating her team like family. To all my fellow sagers, carry on.

I must thank my wife, Tracey, for accepting me as the nerd that I am and listening to me type away during many evenings. And my youngest toddler for letting my brain ponder these little side projects while walking through the bush.

And to my high school friend who showed me what a variable was in Pascal. That was the day I got bit by the programming bug, pun intended. Thanks, mate.

Introduction

Building functional Oracle Application Express (APEX) application is relatively easy. APEX provides many features out-of-the-box that help developers build good applications.

APEX also provides footholds that allow the developer to extend the product with third-party code, producing more polished applications that users feel confident using. A stand-out example of this extensibility are plug-ins, introduced in APEX 4.0.

Another marquee feature introduced in APEX 4.0 is Dynamic Actions. APEX developers whose main skill is typically PL/SQL are now able to declaratively provide more interactive interfaces.

The trouble with Dynamic Actions is that making the most effective use of them requires a deeper understanding of jQuery—the underlying infrastructure that made them tick.

The biggest hurdle with jQuery for PL/SQL developers is the fundamental differences with syntax and semantics. I've met many developers who quickly embraced Dynamic Actions because they saved them from having to learn too much JavaScript, but they only moved into second gear.

After undergoing the same journey myself, I found what I understood to be the secret for Oracle Developers to learning jQuery—building an analogy between CSS and SQL and thus treating the web page like a database.

What This Book Is About

Over the years, I've enjoyed sharing techniques I've learned through my blog and presentations at user group events. However, I felt there was a need in the APEX community to help intermediate APEX developers take their applications to the next level, to use a horrible cliché.

There are some great APEX books out there, but none targeting the use of jQuery within APEX. I'm not aiming to replicate books dedicated to jQuery or JavaScript, rather introduce Oracle technologies to the jQuery syntax and demonstrate how it integrates with APEX.

Many demonstrations in the book are bite-sized, applicable examples that you can start including in your applications tomorrow.

I hope you find this book helpful and that you find a way to share your own discoveries with the development community.

■ **Note** I encourage all readers to engage with the APEX community to help all our applications raise the bar. Participate in forums, blog about your experience, and attend conferences and talk with people.

Who Should Read This Book

You might say this book targets those people just above the beginner level, but it should also appeal to all those wanting to give their users a better experience.

To get the most out of this book, the reader should have a basic familiarity with what seems like a number of technologies, but you may be surprised how well they overlap.

Knowledge of PL/SQL—I'm talking fundamentals here, there is no need to be at the Steven Feuerstein level, but I am using PL/SQL as a device to help the reader pick up jQuery.

Knowledge of SQL—As with PL/SQL I only expect general understanding. I'd like to think developers are always open to expanding their knowledge of both over time.

APEX—Familiarity with APEX. I'm mainly talking about navigating around the Application Builder. Versions differ, and I'll be as specific but general as possible when describing how to apply code. Nobody wants a book with a large percentage of wizard screenshots of an APEX version they don't have when reading the book. APEX 5.0 reduces this issue with its new Page Designer IDE.

HTML—For 90% of the content, only basic understanding of the use of tags such as `<span>` and `<table>` is necessary. Much of the time the type of tag is superfluous; it's just a component in the overall page hierarchy.

CSS—You can copy and paste CSS styling examples straight from this book without needing to understand them, but most style is fairly self-explanatory. This book will teach you how to use CSS selectors target components on the web page.

JavaScript—I would expect this to polarize readers. Some may be able to read or recognize standard syntax, while others may be experienced Oracle APEX plug-in writers who know JavaScript much more intimately than I. The book is about bridging this gap, and I'll walk the reader through what is needed. Knowing how the puzzle pieces in this list relate to each other will go a long way. While reading, you'll learn many of the patterns we regularly use within APEX.

Familiarity with resource materials—On this last point, I'm a big fan of documentation, particularly when it's light. Bookmark the right pages, and you're one click away from 90% of what you'll ever need day-to-day. I have a more comprehensive list in the in the final chapter; the best pages are simple HTML index pages.

For Oracle, I regularly use the SQL Reference manual `https://docs.oracle.com/database/121/SQLRF/toc.htm`.

I use two for jQuery. One is a glossary of selectors: `www.w3schools.com/jquery/jquery_ref_selectors.asp`.

The other is a cheat sheet of functions that point to `api.jquery.com`: `http://oscarotero.com/jquery/`.

Foe most things HTML/CSS-related, I like the simplicity of `w3chools.com`, but I recommend `developer.mozilla.org`.

I also recommend familiarity with Google's search aids that allow you to target certain blogs or forums. Oracle's OTN and stackoverflow is particularly good for jQuery and CSS questions:

`site:community.oracle.com` oracle apex "row template" performance
`site:grassroots-oracle.com` jQuery highlight

▓ **Note**   I encourage all readers to provide me with feedback on any examples you encounter, particularly in relation to how I've applied selectors.

How This Book Is Structured

Part I starts by introducing an analogy that pairs CSS with SQL. The aim is to help Oracle developers familiar with PL/SQL translate these skills into jQuery. It also covers some jQuery fundamentals and the browser tools you'll need to continue the journey.

Part II explores the integration of jQuery with APEX by looking at Dynamic Actions, how they're invoked, and the balance that needs to be found when defining declarative dynamic actions versus writing the equivalent JavaScript.

The ability for the browser to interact with the database is called AJAX. Part III starts detailing this important communication channel by exploring options for invoking PL/SQL processes from the browser, continuing with common patterns used for moving data in APEX applications.

Part IV looks specifically at reporting solutions, starting by adding visualisations to your pages by generating JSON content and sending this to charting libraries. The examples in the book get progressively more difficult, but chapter 14 in particular introduces some more complex JavaScript and jQuery concepts.

Part V finishes the book by describing some other uses for jQuery, illustrating how diverse jQuery techniques can be. These final chapters aim to assist you converting fundamentals learned from the book into more real world scenarios.

The final chapter is a brief introspective based on what has been learned and how it should be applied within APEX. I include some suggestions on what to look out for in the future, since once book can't cover everything. My Journey

I'd like to say a few words about my own career and how I came to the point of writing this book. I completing a computer science degree at university and started as an Oracle Forms and Reports developer who came to understand PL/SQL very well. I then encountered Oracle Portal and mod_plsql, and I started building basic web pages using the htp/htf packages.

Not long after joining Sage Computing Services, I dove into the world of APEX, starting at version 3.1. After numerous blogs, presentations, and forum interaction, I was recognized as an Oracle ACE, but I was still taking very tentative steps into the world of jQuery.

Even today I would not call myself a jQuery expert, but I'm now riding the bike without training wheels, and I'm adapting my techniques as driven by the needs of the applications I'm building.

The decision to write this book was partially borne from the need to refine my skills and seek better practices. It also comes off the back of designing and developing a successful application built specifically for use on a 10" tablet. After dabbling with basic jQuery commands, I was quickly forced to expand my repertoire and start thinking Mobile First. This accelerated my learning curve to a point where I saw a very bright future in the world of web development, but with the awareness that other learning curves are to come.

Figure 1 shows my mental image of the learning in my own career. It's common to think of a learning curve as being a smooth thing, but in reality many of us make large leaps during fits of activity, then calm down and coast for a while, and then experience another large leap. The tablet application was my large leap up the jQuery curve.

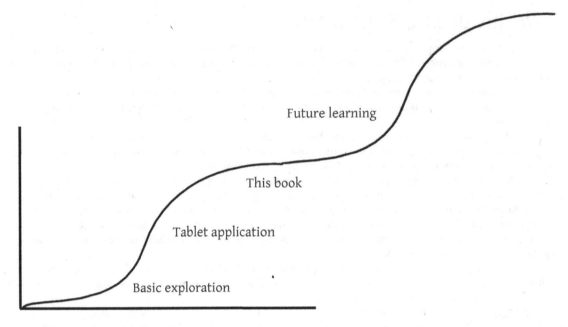

Figure 1. *My jQuery learning curve*

With learning comes awareness, and I now have the fortunate advantage of knowing what the next period of learning might entail. As I start this book I'm leveraging the world of JSON, which is a common lightweight data-interchange format that allows developers to communicate data to contemporary web components such as the following:

- Visualization libraries (Google, Vis.js, D3.js)
- node.js
- angular.js
- LESS/SASS

Understanding these technologies and those that will follow are vital to keeping up with development in the "Internet of Things," the heterogeneous world of smart devices.

Getting Started

To take advantage of the lessons demonstrated in this book, you won't need much more than an Oracle database running APEX 4.x or above, a good browser, and your favorite text editor. The following sections go into more detail on precisely what you'll need.

Oracle Database

To utilize the examples in this book, you'll obviously need an Oracle database running APEX.

There are several options to choose from if you don't already have access to a development environment:

> `apex.oracle.com`: Oracle provides a free online instance of APEX for development purposes. This book was written solely on an instance running in "the cloud," so you should encounter few issues with this option.

> Oracle XE: Oracle also provides a free (for both commercial and personal use) database edition with some size and functional limitations—none of which should impact your ability to learn jQuery. It's a relatively painless way to set up an Oracle instance on your own PC or laptop. An open source project is available to make the process even easier:

> `www.oraopensource.com/oxar/`

> Virtual Machine: Oracle provides a number of virtual machine images with APEX ready to go. All you need is to install Oracle Virtual Box. This means you can get quickly started on whichever operating system you happen to use. These images can be downloaded from the OTN Developer Days page.

APEX Instance

Most examples are fairly independent of the APEX version. You can even run some of these examples on APEX 3.x if you need to. APEX 5.0 was launched while this book was being written and all chapters have differences between 4.x and 5.0 in mind, particularly related to the theme selection.

At the time of writing, the Oracle 11g XE environment came with APEX 4.0.2 pre-installed, which can be upgraded to the 4.2 or the latest 5.0 release.

Development IDE

Most of the examples in this book require such little code that they can be easily included inline within the APEX page attributes or Dynamic Actions. Ultimately it is better practice to contain such code within their own CSS and JS files, so I recommend using your favorite text editor.

Free editors are available such as Atom or Notepad++, and others such as TextPad and Sublime have nominal license fees.

Oracle provides a free PL/SQL and SQL IDE called SQL Developer. As per text editors, SQL Developer provides syntax highlighting and allows you to browse database objects and debug code. Other third-party tools are available such as Toad or PL/SQL Developer.

Web Browser

APEX officially supports relatively recent versions of the four major browsers— IE, Firefox, Chrome, and Safari. Screenshots used in the examples in this book use Chrome as I personally find this the easiest browser to inspect under the hood of the web page. Safari is quite similar, and Firefox with the Firebug extension provides the same type of functionality.

Web Server

A web server is the gateway that allows your browser to communicate to the database and typically serve JavaScript and CSS files to the browser. As part of the APEX installation process, some form of web server will have been set up, but you don't need to place external files on the server to try the book's examples. Best practice suggests this is done in a production instance, but deeper discussions on this topic have previously been covered elsewhere and are beyond the intended scope of this book.

APEX Application

Finally, you'll need an APEX application on which to experiment and try out the examples. The examples in this book only need a simple framework of pages to get started. In fact, most of the examples are based on a classic report page or an accompanying form. Others will require a basic page with a HTML region and a few buttons.

I will start with a database application using the default options in the Create Application wizard:

1. Desktop User Interface

2. Include Home Page

3. Universal Theme (Theme 42)

I will use the EMP table found in the sample SCOTT schema that comes with the default database install, but any table will do—,and that's the point. There is no reason why you can't translate the examples found in this book to your own data model.

No doubt the exact wizard process will change over time, but once you've decided what table to use, create a new page selecting the following:

1. Form

2. Form on a Table with Report

3. Implementation "Classic" (not Interactive) with a "Reports Region" template

4. Page and region labeled "Employees"

5. Select the EMP table

6. Create a new navigation menu entry under Home

7. Accept remaining defaults for the report

8. Set the form to use Primary Key column EMPNO (as opposed to Manage by Database ROWID)

9. Use any existing sequence to populate the primary key

10. Include all available columns in the form

You should end up with an application with four pages as shown in Figure 2.

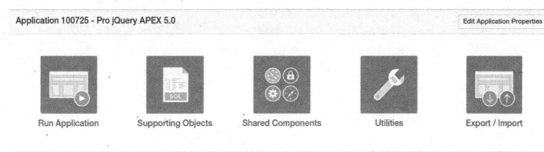

Figure 2. *Suggested application page framework*

Some chapters will build on these pages, while others will suggest you create a fresh page. There are no prerequisite chapters for any examples, though I recommend reading the first six chapters before skipping ahead to any practical examples.

Most examples could be applied to any theme, but Chapters 4 and 17 specifically mention Theme 25. This is due in part since some examples aren't really required in the Universal Theme, but past themes will remain in use for some time. Realistically, it's mostly class names that change between themes.

All examples can be easily translated to your own pages in your own applications, which is the concept I want to iterate. This book aims to raise awareness of the capabilities of jQuery libraries and then show you how easily it can be adopted to the APEX environment.

In the spirit of a social media mantra engineered by Joel Kallman,

`#letswreckthistogether.`

PART I

Getting Started

CHAPTER 1

∎ ∎ ∎

CSS—The Secret

You may wonder what a chapter about Cascading Style Sheets (CSS) is doing at the beginning of a book about jQuery. In fact, I didn't fully understand the connection until I drew the analogy between SQL and jQuery. CSS selectors locate web page elements in a way analogous to the where clause of a SQL statement.

This chapter aims to help you understand this analogy and show you how to leverage your existing SQL skills to locate page elements for jQuery to act upon. jQuery turns the analogy into a SQL update, and JavaScript (where jQuery expressions live) has translations to PL/SQL.

First, you'll see how selectors work and how you can use them to identify components of a web page, just like you do with data in SQL. The chapter then describes events that can be placed on these selectors, finishing the analogy by comparing JavaScript to PL/SQL.

Understanding the Selector

Before diving deeply into how the selector works, let's look at how the web page is structured, see some basic syntax examples, and explore the SQL analogy.

Fundamentally, it comes back to CSS selectors identifying page elements. Sizzle.js is the engine that powers the jQuery library, and it extends the number of selectors available to provide more granular access to elements on the page. jQuery extends this further by traversing the tree that represents the web page, and visiting and acting upon a set of specified elements.

The Web Page Is Hierarchical Data

jQuery is a Document Object Model (DOM) manipulation library. What is a DOM? It's an object model that describes the logical structure of HTML (and XML) documents, and how they're accessed and manipulated.

The web page shown in Figure 1-1 and the underlying HTML in Listing 1-1 can be represented as a tree. This web page will be used for coding examples throughout Part 1.

Figure 1-1. *The sample page (also supplied as sample.html)*

Listing 1-1. Sample web page – sample.html

```
<HTML>
  <HEAD><TITLE>My home page</TITLE></HEAD>
  <BODY>
    <H1 id="demo1">jQuery Demos</H1>
    <P>Let me tell you about my favorite science communicators:
    <UL id="communicators">
      <LI> Carl Sagan
      <LI> Neil deGrasse Tyson
      <LI> Eugenie Scott
    </UL>
  </BODY>
</HTML>
```

■ **Note**   The actual source contains a little bit more code that does not affect the tree representation, but has been omitted for clarity.

The web page in Figure 1-1 can be mapped into a tree, as shown in Figure 1-2, though you might visualize it sideways, as shown in the indented code. The HTML element is the hierarchical parent of all the nodes. The list elements become siblings, all children to UL, grandchildren to BODY, and so on.

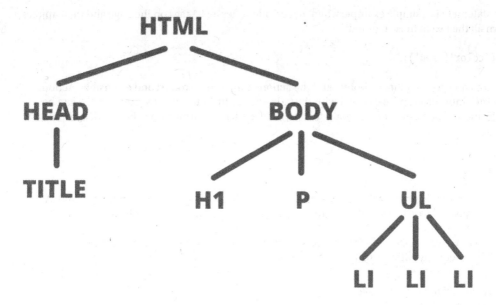

Figure 1-2. *jQuery traverses this tree to apply functions*

jQuery syntax is represented as `$(selector).action()`, and the elements selector component can be used to identify parts of this tree. Attributes such as ID and CLASS can be used to filter specific nodes on the document tree. The selectors used within the $ function are exactly why jQuery can be likened to SQL, with further detail on that in the "SQL Analogy" section later in the chapter.

HTML, CSS & jQuery Syntax Examples

Once upon a time the main function of CSS was to provide a presentation overlay for a HTML page. Consider a need to turn all H1 level HTML headings on the sample page to a red font.

```
<h1>jQuery Demos</h1>
```

CSS would use a selector to locate the page elements and then apply the relevant markup during the page render, which reduces the repetition required to format an entire web site.

CSS is typically located either within a .css file included in the HTML page or as an inline style. The following CSS uses the h1 element as the selector pattern to find any h1 tags on a web page and then sets the color attribute as red:

```
h1 {
  color : red;
}
```

You can apply these attributes on demand with a click of a button. Everything in jQuery is done via the $() factory function, extended to `$(selector).action();`.

The next statement is a simple example where jQuery identifies all h1 tags on the page and then applies the CSS to turn all the text in those tags red:

```
$('h1').css('color','red');
```

The selector can become more elaborate and the actions can become robust and extensible. Actions such as .fadeIn() introduce a page element with the fade effect. Attributes such as ID and CLASS can be used to identify more specific elements of your document. The trick to learning how they work is comparing selectors to SQL.

SQL Analogy

The best science communicators are those that find brilliant analogies that a layman can understand. As database technologists, we are lucky that SQL provides us the perfect analogy for how jQuery modifies elements within a web page.

Visualizing a web page, as shown in Figure 1-2, is the first step to understanding how this translates to SQL. Now compare that hierarchy with the rows in Table 1-1.

Table 1-1. *Records within the EMP Table*

ID	NAME	SALARY
100	SCOTT	5000
102	KYLIE	4000
102	EDDIE	3500
103	PENNY	8000

To update SCOTT and improve his salary, the SQL statement identifies which row to update and then changes the value of the column. For example, if you want to update a record in the database, you would run a SQL statement like the following:

```
UPDATE employees
SET salary = salary * 1.5
WHERE name = 'SCOTT';
```

This statement locates the employee named SCOTT and adds 50% to the salary. Table 1-2 shows a representation of the employees table and example data.

Table 1-2. *Records within the EMP Table*

ID	NAME	SALARY
100	SCOTT	5000
102	KYLIE	4000
102	EDDIE	3500
103	PENNY	8000

Compare the SQL statement with the following jQuery statement that locates a h1 tag with the ID 'demo1' and update the displayed text:

```
$('body h1#demo1').text('Hello Universe');
```

compares to the use of unique key indexes in SQL. This means there can be good, inefficient, and potentially erroneous. The description of what the two statements do is similar. The following pseudo-SQL demonstrates how the jQuery statement can be represented as a SQL statement. Even the use of an ID element usage of selectors:

```
UPDATE html_page
SET text = 'Hello Universe'
WHERE id = 'demo1'
AND tag = 'h1';
```

Even the string literal is case sensitive, as it would be in the database.

Parallels between the two languages are summarized in Figure 1-3. The comparison is not exact as jQuery offers a number of facilities for traversing nodes of the tree that don't translate to SQL, but it shows the syntax isn't as foreign as it may first appear.

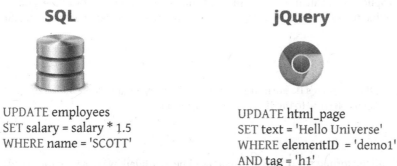

Figure 1-3. *The SQL analogy*

Understanding Selectors

Selectors are patterns that match tags and attributes to the HTML markup itself. Many are fundamental to the CSS core, the Sizzle.js engine under $() provides extends selectors with more advanced features and capabilities.

Selectors also represent the WHERE clause of the SQL analogy, so we need to understand their capabilities and also consider that poorly written jQuery can affect browser performance.

Once you understand selectors, you understand jQuery. If you can identify the page elements you want to change, you can apply any of a diverse set of functions to it. It will be like riding a bike—once you know how, you want to go exploring.

■ **Tip**   A concise reference to jQuery selectors can be found at the following address: www.w3schools.com/jquery/jquery_ref_selectors.asp.

Tags, IDs, and Classes

The sample page offers two options to locate the h1 tag. All HTML tags can be identified by name, and hierarchy can be signified within the selector. Any h1 tags within a bodynode would be returned using the following:

```
$('body h1')
```

The other option is to use the element's ID attribute to uniquely identify a page element. For example, you can identify a specific element referring to the ID using the # symbol:

```
$('#demo1')
```

Classes are identified with the format tag.class. The class can be identified by itself with the .coolCat dot notation. However, to aid performance in many cases, it's recommended to precede it with the HTML tag that would have that class. This selector locates any list items with the coolCat class.

```
li.coolCat
```

■ **Tip**   ID and class selectors are case sensitive, as per the string comparisons in the SQL. Tags, however, tolerate either case.

Attributes and Operator

It's possibly to identify elements by other attributes. A common example I use in APEX is to look in a report identified with the id p2_emps and locate any cells for the ENAME column:

```
#p2_emps td[headers='ENAME']
```

This translates to the HTML typically generated for APEX classic report data columns:

```
<td headers="ENAME">
```

The earlier example of h1#demo1 could also be written in a similar way, but classes and IDs have their own identifiers so the shortened form can be used instead:

```
h1[id="demo1"]
```

Searching for attribute values becomes more flexible with operator extensions similar to % and _ wildcards in SQL. The tilde in the following example looks for attributes beginning with the string "DATE". As a result, the invocation of jQuery targets APEX columns such as DATE_CALLED, DATE_MODIFIED, and so forth:

```
td[headers^="DATE"]
```

Pseudo-Selectors

Pseudo-selectors are used to identify information that is not in the document tree. A common example you may have seen is :hover, typically applied on an anchor tag in the form a:hover.

Examples specific to jQuery include tr:even, to get all the even tr elements; or :contains('wesley'), to return all those elements containing my name as text. Specific siblings such as list items in an unordered list can be identified positionally like an array:

```
$("ul li:eq(1)")
```

■ **Tip**   Web sites such as caniuse.com help determine why certain CSS or HTML tags are not recognized in your browser. IE has a history of lagging behind in support due to longer release cycles.

Browser Feedback

You can ask your browser to provide immediate feedback as to how accurate your selectors are by opening the browser's Developer Tools JavaScript console. Do that by pressing Ctrl-Shift-J or F12, through the browser menu, or via Inspect Element when right-clicking within the page. Figure 1-4 shows the sample page with the Developer Tools docked to the bottom with the console tab shown. I manually entered **$('h1')** and the console returned the array of results.

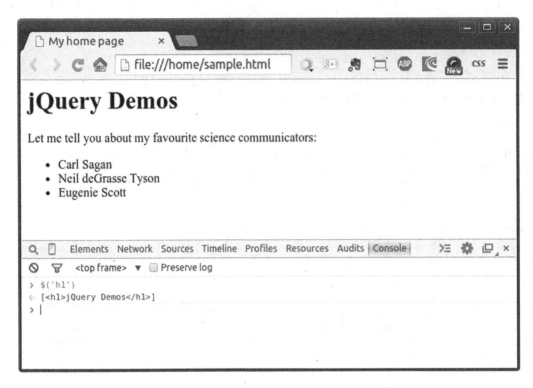

Figure 1-4. Chrome JavaScript console window

Events

DOM selection and manipulation in jQuery is essential for identifying web page components. Event handling facilitates interaction with these identified components by the end users by responding to their input devices.

Touch screens have turned the user's fingers into input devices and events such as those responding to gestures are handled specifically with jQueryMobile—a framework for creating mobile applications. APEX applications don't *need* to include the mobile framework to handle standard tap and scrolling events. A small library called *Touch Punch* can be included on a web page to make it respond to dragging gestures, useful for slider items.

If you've ever defined a dynamic action on change of an item, you have applied an event listener to your page. APEX provides the ability to define these events and subsequent actions declaratively. This book gradually explores the balance between jQuery and dynamic actions.

To call a function as a result of an event on the page, define a listener for a given selector. The following example calls myFunction on a click (or touch) on the page component with id demo1:

```
('#demo1').on('click', myFunction);
```

Functions invoked like this are called *callbacks* and will have access to contextual event information. This information allows the code to make decisions based on the current state of the web page. This book will demonstrate a number of examples applicable to the APEX environment.

Other major event types include on load of the page, before/after refresh of report regions, and gesturing events similar to mouse interactions such as touchstart and touchend.

A proportion of PL/SQL developers will also be familiar with Oracle Forms—a development IDE now superseded by jDeveloper ADF and APEX. Web page events can draw further analogies to Oracle Forms events as mapped in Table 1-3.

Table 1-3. *Forms Events and Their JavaScript Equivalent*

Forms	JavaScript
when-new-form-instance	load
when-validate-item	change
when-mouse-click when-button-pressed	click
pre-query	beforerefresh
when-mouse-down	touchstart

Translating PL/SQL to JavaScript

The analogy connecting selectors to CSS doesn't just extend to events. Table 1-4 and Table 1-5 respectively map the syntax and data structures between PL/SQL and JavaScript.

Table 1-4. *Typical PL/SQL Expressions and Their JavaScript Equivalent*

	PL/SQL	JavaScript
concat	'Hello '||'Universe'	'Hello '+"Universe"
Built-ins	UPPER('Hello')	"Hello".toUpperCase()
length	LENGTH('Hello')	"Hello".length
conversion	2 = TO_NUMBER(2)	2 == parseInt("2")
Variables	planet VARCHAR2(20) := 'Earth';	var planet = 'Earth';
Output	dbms_output.put_line(planet);	console.log(planet);
If boolean	If 1 = 2 then end if;	if (1==2) { }
Null function	COALESCE(planet, 'Mars')	planet == '' ? 'Mars' : planet

Table 1-5. *Forms Events and Their JavaScript Equivalent*

	PL/SQL	JavaScript
records	Me person%ROWTYPE; me.name := 'Scott'; me.vintage := 1979;	var me = { name : "Scott" ,vintage : 1979 } console.log(me.name);
arrays	type t_array is varray(3) of number; v_array t_array; v_array := t_array(1, 2, 3);	var y = [1, 2, 3] y[0] == 1 // true
loops	for rec in 1..v_array.count loop dbms_output.put_line('val:'||v_array(rec)); end loop;	For { var i=0; i<y.length; i++) { console. log('val:'+y[i]); }
functions	Function do_something(p_id number) return number is begin ... end;	function do_something(p_id) { ... }

Note strings in JavaScript can use either single or double quotation marks to bound the string, and nested strings can use alternating quotes:

```
$("#p2_emps td[headers='ENAME']")
```

Nulls are handled by JavaScript in its own peculiar way. It's worth researching their behaviors in media more specific to JavaScript itself. There are plenty of references available online for handling nulls in any language.

JavaScript will also accept your concatenation attempt if you used 'Hello'||"Universe", though the double pipe will be treated as an OR boolean expression and will only return the string 'Hello':

```
apex.debug('p1_value: ' || p1_value);
```

This slip up can make debugging harder as this expression is syntactically valid but will always return a string that makes the parameter look empty:

What's Available from the Box?

jQuery has been included by default in APEX applications since the advent of dynamic actions. The application builder provided wizards to define event handlers that interact with page components.

In addition to dynamic actions, APEX provides the ability to utilize other jQuery features declaratively. For instance, date pickers and autocomplete items use the jQuery framework. Many types of APEX plug-ins also use the jQuery library to function.

APEX also provides a number of JavaScript APIs that wrap interactions that seem specific to APEX, or emulate SQL style functions, such as $nvl() or $v(). Details on these can be found in the APEX API reference documentation.

To keep the amount of JavaScript required to service the typical web page low, a number of jQuery functions aren't included by default.

APEX does include the necessary libraries in the /images folder. To include support for slider bars, type the following in the page attribute *JavaScript File URLs*:

```
#IMAGE_PREFIX#libraries/jquery-ui/1.8/ui/minified/jquery.ui.slider.min.js
```

You can even include the jQuery core library in APEX 3.x and take advantage of examples in this book.

All this means you can start utilizing jQuery functionality straight away in versions APEX 4.x and up.

Summary

Oracle developers shouldn't find themselves in a chasm when exploring the use of jQuery. A basic jQuery command breaks down into two components, the first of which can be equated to the WHERE clause of a SQL statement. The second is the function that applies the relevant effect or triggers a process.

Document manipulation and event handling are not only marquee components of the jQuery framework, but are also fundamental to supporting effects and animations, AJAX, and data communication using the JSON format. jQuery also provides extensibility through plug-ins. All these features will be explored in later chapters.

CHAPTER 2

■ ■ ■

jQuery Fundamentals

Mastering the concept of selectors is a difficult part of learning jQuery. There are a number of methods to identify the right page element to act upon. In addition to the selectors mentioned in Chapter 1, jQuery also provides the ability to traverse up and down the HTML tree using specific functions.

More detailed examples of selectors will be introduced as the chapter details traversal methods in addition to other fundamental concepts and common features. Just like SQL, a good percentage of what you'll ever need to do will already have an appropriate documented function.

This book mostly focuses on jQuery within APEX, but this chapter will help you find your bearings in the new language. This chapter ends by introducing AJAX as the bridge to communicate with the database.

To get a deeper understanding of jQuery, I would recommend a book dedicated to the topic. *Pro jQuery*, by Adam Freeman (Apress), provides a comprehensive introduction to the jQuery language.

Including jQuery in Your Page

For simplicity, the `sample.html` page introduced in Chapter 1 includes code that was not originally shown. Listing 2-1 shows how a recent version of the jQuery library from a Content Delivery Network (CDN) can be included on any page, in addition to a style definition used in the following examples.

Listing 2-1 Extend Sample Page to Include jQuery and Styling

```
<script type="text/javascript"
            src="https://code.jquery.com/jquery-1.11.1.js"></script>
<style>
.coolCat {
  font-weight:bold;
}
</style>
```

The supplied sample page places it between the closing body and HTML tags. The exact placement of this code isn't that important for a sample page like this one; HTML is interpreted with great tolerance by many of the browsers. Normally, style content is placed in the HEAD tag, or preferably included as a `.css` style sheet file separate from the HTML document.

The best placement for script content changes over time, but the current rule of thumb is to place or include files near the closing BODY tag.

The examples in this chapter can be applied to the sample page via browser console, as shown in Figure 2-1. The text with greater-than symbol (>) prefixes is what I typed into the console. From APEX 4.0, pages have core jQuery libraries built in.

13

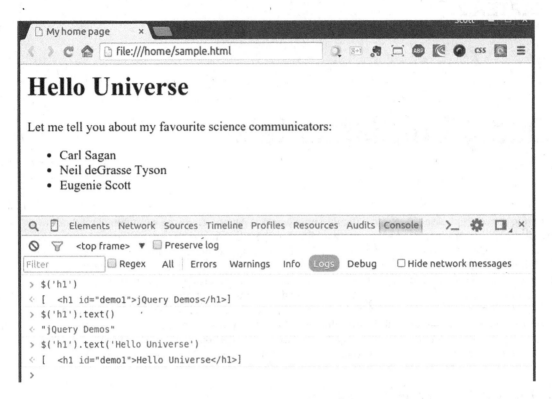

Figure 2-1. *Your first jQuery commands run in the browser console*

Getting and Setting

The "Hello Universe" example in the SQL analogy used in Chapter 1 introduced a jQuery function that sets a value. Typically, the types of functions that access attributes of page elements are overloaded such that they will either show the current value of the specified attribute of those elements or set it if a parameter is passed.

Often the difference between getting and setting a value is the presence of a parameter. The first command in the following example gets a value. The second command sets the attribute to the actual parameter value that is passed.

Enter the following commands in the Console tab and consider the output:

```
$('h1').text();
$('h1').text('Hello Universe');
```

In this case, the attribute is the text within the h1 element. Classes and height/width dimensions can also be manipulated with jQuery.

The sample page will also includes a simple CSS class called coolCat that will apply boldness to any text with that class. For example:

```
<li class="coolCat"> Neil deGrasse Tyson
```

jQuery provides the ability to apply the same attribute in response to whatever event you require. To apply this class to all list item elements, use the .addClass() function. The selector is the LI tag, indicating all such tags within the page. The function's parameter indicates the class name to add to the selected element:

```
$('li').addClass('coolCat');
```

The following are get/set functions you might find used within an APEX environment. You'll see some of them used in examples throughout the book.

- attr()
- prop()
- data()
- is()
- css()
- removeClass()
- toggleClass()
- height()
- width()

Traversing

jQuery provides a number of functions that allow you to traverse the DOM. This means that when starting at one selector, you can move up the tree representing the web page, and down the tree, or even sideways across list elements or table rows and cells.

Before you start traversing the DOM, it is good practice to specify the appropriate set of elements or starting point. For instance, there may be more than one unordered list on a page, so specify the list with the ID of the list in the selector:

```
$('#communicators li')
```

Siblings

The items inside the #communicators list are considered siblings to each other. To specify certain nodes within a set of siblings such as list elements, a number of pseudo-selectors is available. These pseudo-selectors can be applied within the selector or using jQuery functions defined for traversing.

To return the first list item in a set, you would use the selector :first. However, you could also use the jQuery function first(). This means the following statements return Carl Sagan, though performance may vary:

```
$('#communicators li:first').text()
$('#communicators li').first().text()
```

```
Carl Sagan
```

To honor Neil deGrasse Tyson's former dancing skills and make him the the `coolCat` while leaving everyone else normal, jQuery can identify a specific element in the list. The items in the list can be treated like an array with the function `eq()`, where the parameter is the position within the array:

```
$('#communicators li:eq(1)').addClass('coolCat');
```

Like JavaScript, arrays start counting from zero. Tyson is the second name in the list, and thus we refer to him via the index value 1.

Using the `coolCat` class as the selector that identifies Tyson, return the set of list item siblings with the following snippet:

```
$('.coolCat').siblings()
```

```
[<li>Carl Sagan</li>, <li>Eugenie Scott</li>]
```

Ancestry

The terminology used in traversing up and down the tree is the same as you'd use for your family. In our sample page, we can start from UL using `#communicators`, or from the second list item with the class attributed to Neil Tyson using `li.coolCat`.

List items are descendants of `#communicators`, accessible using functions like `children()` and `find()`. For example, you can retrieve the text of the list items in `#communicators` as follows:

```
$('#communicators').children()
```

```
[<li>Carl Sagan</li>,<li class="coolCat">Neil Tyson</li>,<li>Eugenie Scott</li>]
```

The next example finds any elements underneath `#communicators` with the class `.coolCat`. This might be the next level under as in the sample page, or it could be any number of nodes deep.

```
$('#communicators').find('.coolCat')
```

```
[<li class="coolCat">Neil Tyson</li>]
```

When moving up the tree using functions `closest()` and `parent()`, the latter takes one step up the tree at a time while the former will look for selectors anywhere in the ancestry, similar to `find()`.

I prefer `closest()` as it's less likely to break when the page is modified. If the target node is a few levels higher, it saves chaining a number of `parent()` together. More on chaining in the next section.

Here jQuery starts at any list elements with the class `.coolCat`, and then traverses up to the closest unordered list. In this case, `parent()` would accomplish the same task.

```
$('.coolCat').closest('ul')
```

```
[<ul id="communicators">...</ul>]
```

Then you can move up another level with .parent():

```
$('.coolCat').closest('ul').parent()
```

```
[<body>...</body>]
```

BODY and HTML are considered ancestors to everything underneath them. In our example page, the unnumbered list is immediately inside the HTML body. That's why the BODY tag is returned as the parent of the list.

These examples show jQuery and selectors can be interchanged in a number of different ways to identify elements of the page. Finding the right balance can be difficult, particularly when learning. Some will perform better, while others will seem more elegant. I'll do my best to show the methods I've found that work best for me in the given situation.

■ **Note**   Like PL/SQL, you will find selectors provide a number of ways to achieve the same task. We all find ways to refine and improve our techniques as we learn. I'm happy to receive feedback on snippets you find in this book, particularly those considering performance.

Chaining

Chaining is a natural part of jQuery that is utilized frequently to run multiple jQuery methods on the same element with a single statement. This could be likened to updating multiple columns in a SQL update statement.

To add the class to Tyson and shorten his name, use a jQuery function to identify the node.

Instead of executing two separate statements—one to add a class and another to set the text—we can *chain* the commands for efficiency and readability. Chaining simply means adding multiple function notation calls to the selector. For example, to add the class to Tyson and shorten his name, you would use the following:

```
$('#communicators li').eq(1).addClass('coolCat').text('Neil Tyson');
```

For readability—particularly with longer chains—you can format the statement over multiple lines, just like in SQL:

```
$('#communicators li')
  .eq(1)
  .addClass('coolCat')
  .text('Neil Tyson');
```

The selector supplied to jQuery locates all list items within #communicators, and then filters the list to just the second element. The class is then added and the element text modified.

The browser takes longer to complete the actions if written as multiple statements. jQuery needs to locate the selector each time, and it won't have the advantage of Oracle's optimization techniques for frequently accessed information. Therefore, the following two statements will take longer to complete than the previous chained example:

```
$('#communicators li:eq(1)').addClass('coolCat')
$('#communicators li:eq(1)').text('Neil Tyson');
```

Effects

The term *effect* in jQuery refers to what you want to have happen to the elements you've selected. Simple, yet effective effects can be applied to whatever selector is used.

Some jQuery examples with obvious outcomes include the functions .hide() and .show(). These effects set the display property of the selected elements to none, as in display: none.

You may have already utilized these effects with the corresponding APEX JavaScript APIs $x_Show() and $x_Hide(). Other APIs also exist to traverse the tree. One example similar to .closest(), is $x_UpTill().

Other methods provide animated effects, such as .slideDown() and .fadeOut().

Visit the API documentation to determine the parameters available to these functions that I've mentioned. For example, find the parameters to .slideDown() at the following URL:

http://api.jquery.com/slidedown/

The URL pattern is consistent. Replace slidedown in the URL with hide or show or the name of any other function of interest.

Alternatively, you get help by quickly googling the function name, as in "jquery slidedown."

Figure 2-2 shows the start of what is a concise documentation format; it's the documentation for .slideDown. Further down the page are details regarding available options along with a simple description of what the function does with a basic example of the function in action.

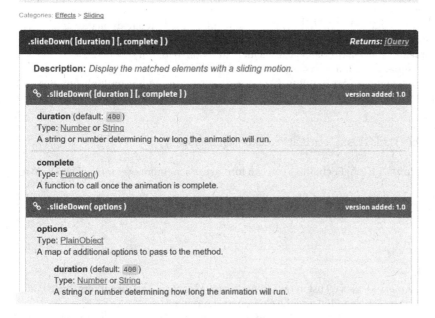

Figure 2-2. *jQuery documentation for slideDown()*

Sometimes related functions can be mentioned and linked to, particularly if deprecation has occurred with a newer release of jQuery.

Callbacks

Note the description for the `complete` parameter in Figure 2-2. It's a function that's called once the animation task has completed. These types of functions are called *callbacks*. They are used frequently within the jQuery framework to ensure processes are executed only upon successful completion of the task.

Statements are processed in JavaScript without regard to whether the prior statement has been executed. In this case, process B will start before process A may have finished:

processA;

processB;

Callbacks can ensure process B is only executed once process A finishes, typically by passing the second function as a parameter to the first.

AJAX Callbacks

There is another type of callback, known as an AJAX callback, that allows us to call PL/SQL. AJAX callbacks allow us to communicate between the JavaScript and database world.

Later in the book, I'll go into further detail about the syntax variations available to bridge the gap between the browser and the database, but for now I want to mention the two main methods of invoking PL/SQL from the web page: dynamic actions and jQuery wrappers.

Dynamic Actions

You've actually defined an AJAX callback if you've ever defined a dynamic action that fires some PL/SQL as the result of some interaction on the page. APEX provides a declarative format to execute these calls, but JavaScript can provide added flexibility in more complex scenarios, in part since APEX doesn't facilitate conditional actions.

Figure 2-3 shows an APEX dynamic action invoking PL/SQL. APEX 5.0 also kindly indicates my sample function does not exist in the database. The `Page Items to Submit` attribute indicates which items need values sent from the web page to session state in the database. Comma separated items in `Page Items to Return` will list which page items should be updated to reflect value from session state.

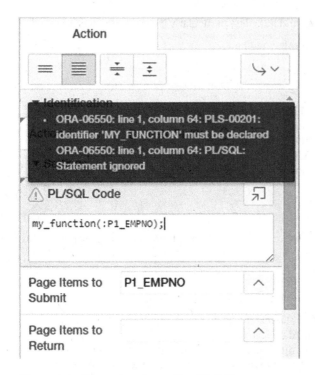

Figure 2-3. Dynamic action calling PL/SQL

APEX jQuery Wrapper

The same PL/SQL in the dynamic action can be invoked using JavaScript. In fact, APEX converts dynamic actions to just that. The next example is representative of what APEX generates to serve the dynamic action. Instead, this case invokes PL/SQL in an AJAX callback called "MY_CALLBACK." It will also set the PL/SQL package variable apex_application.g_x01 to whatever value is found in the browser for item P1_EMPNO. From APEX 5 this information is also accessible using substitution strings APP_AJAX_01 through APP_AJAX_10.

```
apex.server.process("MY_CALLBACK"
  , {x01 : $v('P1_EMPNO')}
).done(function(pData) {
  /* pData returned from database using htp package or proxy */
});
```

Embedding this as JavaScript provides advantages such as the ability to execute only under specific conditions in a workflow. It will call certain code upon success or failure. Attributes APEX provides declaratively are available as optional parameters, further explored in Chapter 9 on processes.

Summary

jQuery is not that complicated. All you need to do is identify the part of the web page to update with a selector and then apply a function to that page element.

You can chain functions together, applying all to the selected elements. You can also traverse the tree in any direction from a given selector, perhaps locating a key node from a click event further down the tree.

Most importantly, you can execute PL/SQL on demand from within JavaScript and pass information back and forth. This allows an integration between the browser and database that enriches the user interfaces by minimizing the amount of entire page submissions required.

CHAPTER 3

Browser Tools

Familiarity with the browser is vital to a pain-free experience while tinkering with CSS and jQuery. Even though browsers have a lot of cousins, certain tools are common to many and will be useful while you apply examples from the book.

This will be the final chapter in Part 1, "Getting Started." In Part 2, we will move on to APEX for context-specific examples.

Chrome vs. the Rest

Once during a presentation, I showed a slide that stated, "Use Chrome or go home." That slide got quite the reaction at the time, and I've had a few comments since. I'm sure most developers have their preference in browsers, and we've all heard the jokes about Internet Explorer (IE).

Chrome is a clear leader for web developers, with Firefox now a distant but clear second. Chrome also happens to be my preference, so the examples and screenshots in this book will be Chrome. Chrome is a light browser that includes everything a web developer needs straight out of the box. Other browsers will have their own equivalent features.

Developer Tools

Open any web page in Chrome and press F12. Doing so will open up the browser tools that can be used to look under the proverbial hood of any web page. Figure 3-1 shows what these tools look like.

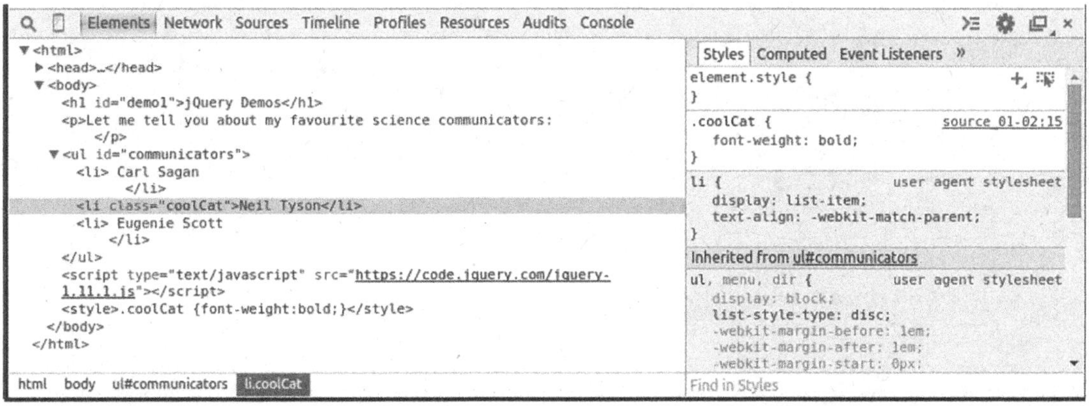

Figure 3-1. *Chrome browser tools*

Other means to the same end include pressing Ctrl-Shift-J or right clicking within the web page and selecting Inspect Element.

Most modern browsers include some form of browser tools off the shelf. Extensions also exist that offer similar functionality and other features. This chapter covers the major functions you're likely to frequent.

▪ **Caution** While Chrome may be useful for development, be sure to test your site across all browsers and major versions.

Exploring the Contents of Your Page

To inspect the properties of the list item for Neil Tyson, the quickest method would be to right click his name on the web page and choose Inspect Element. Doing so will open the browser's developer tools (if not already open) and show the Elements panel.

You'll spend much of your time within developer tools jumping between the Elements and Console panels. Depending on how big your display is, it's useful to split the windows using the Show Drawer icon. That's the fourth icon from top-right, shaded blue in Figure 3-2. The split window allows you to write and test JavaScript while reviewing the internals of the page. Alternatively, you can undock the tools from the web page.

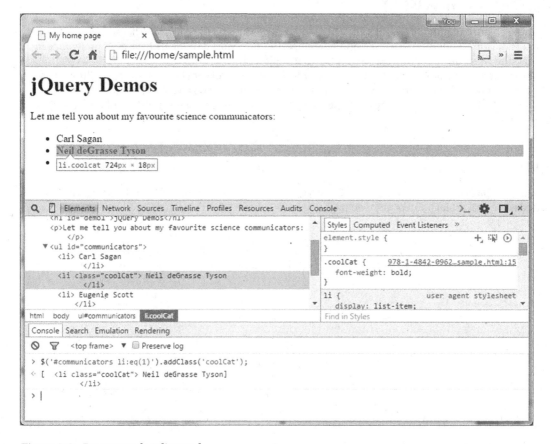

Figure 3-2. *Browser tools split panel*

The Elements panel illustrates the Document Object Model (DOM) tree. Bear in mind this tree is not necessarily what was generated from APEX, nor is it the original source from a static HTML file. Consider that the DOM is a live representation of the web page after the browser has processed the source and any jQuery interactions have also been applied.

The fact that the browser renders based on the DOM also means developers have the ability to manipulate the page and see the effects on the page straight away. In the Elements panel we can add, modify, or remove nodes from the DOM. We could right click the <h1> tag and remove the node, edit the ID attribute, or add another attribute.

■ **Tip**　More detailed information on how to use Chrome's developer tools can be found at developer.chrome.com.

Styles

The Styles panel is ideal for testing CSS manipulations of a page. The Styles panel enables developers to do the following:

- Identify where certain styles have come from, which could be the APEX template, your project's CSS or plug-in, inline CSS, or applied programmatically with jQuery

- See styles with lower CSS specificity that were overlooked and determine from which CSS files, which can help developers determine where code needs to reside

- Add your own attributes on the fly, often to test their location and effectiveness before applying within the page's infrastructure

- Toggle element state, activating states such as :hover without the cursor needing to be physically hovering over the element

Computed

The Computed panel is the place to look when you simply want to know the derived values of certain attributes and where they came from. This panel consolidates the list shown in the Styles panel, detailing the style each attribute utilized. Expanding each attribute will show which source was used, and list those with lower precedence struck out underneath.

Figure 3-3 shows how a selected element is represented in the CSS Box Model. Any margin, border, or padding is shown. Associated colors are replicated on the web page when the mouse hovers over the node in the Elements panel. You can also see the resultant dimensions of the element.

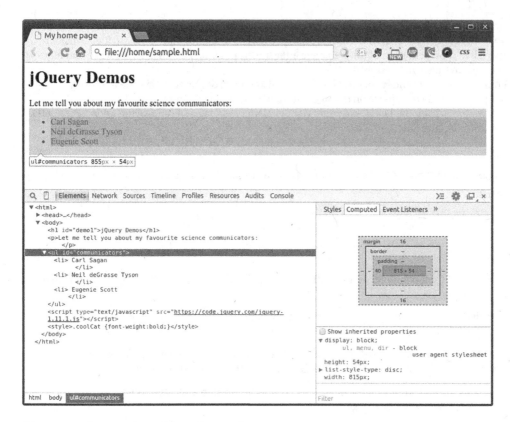

Figure 3-3. *Computed panel for web page elements*

Event Listeners

The sample page has no event listeners to display. However, when there are event listeners present, use the panel of that same name to view them. This panel will be useful for examples later in the book.

Add a basic event listener on the sample page by executing the following code in the Console panel. Then refresh the Event Listeners tab to see a click event added to ul#communicators.

```
$('ul').on('click', function() {console.log(this)});
```

If you don't see the click event shown in the Event Listeners tab, ensure the UL tag is selected in the Elements tab.

Console

Click the Console tab to view the Console panel. Use the JavaScript console to monitor messages and feedback from the browser. Also use it to execute JavaScript and test jQuery selectors and commands on the fly. This book enables you to use the console to test jQuery selectors and look for instrumentation messages sent from JavaScript using the console.log() debugging function.

There are other methods available in the console object, which is a non-standard package not suitable for production in all browsers—particularly not in older versions of IE. The console object is a great debugging tool, however. And for APEX development, you can utilise apex.debug(), which will only write to the console if debugging is enabled for the current page, using code relevant to the current browser.

■ **Tip** There is an open source console wrapper designed specifically for APEX. It's available at https://github.com/OraOpenSource/Logger.

Mobile Emulator

The Chrome Device Mode and Emulation panel is a brilliant resource for testing your pages against mobile devices. Figure 3-3 shows the browser with the emulator turned on using the smartphone icon, which is found between the search icon and Elements tab.

Chrome allows you to specify the device you would like to emulate from a decent range of contemporary devices. This viewport can be easily scaled to suit whatever monitor you're using.

Other features include a network throttler to simulate access speeds on a mobile network. The Emulation tab can specify the media type used to render. Select *Print* as your CSS media type to see how your page may change when printed.

The cursor also changes from the standard arrow to a semi-translucent circle. This indicates the behavior will emulate the finger on a touchscreen. Touch and drag emulate perfectly—certain features will not work on a browser without touch awareness defined on the page. More noticeable is the scrolling drift when vertically scrolling large pages. Such drift is not present in a desktop environment. Figure 3-4 illustrates Chrome emulating my current smartphone size in portrait.

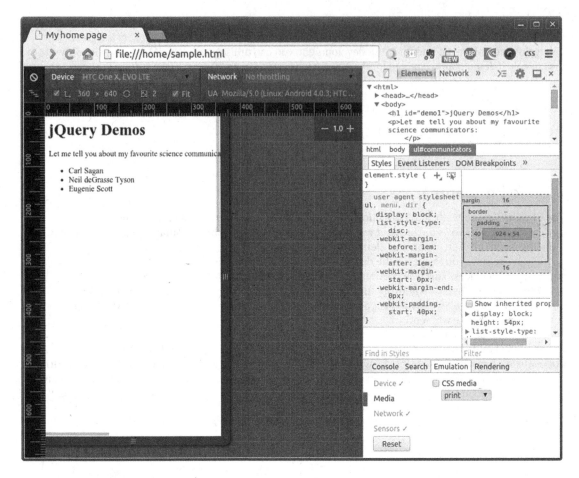

Figure 3-4. *Chrome Mobile Emulator*

Summary

The Chrome browser stands out when comparing standard built-in features to the other major players. This doesn't mean you can't use your favorite browser's developer tools—they all do the same job and may have improved since I developed my browser preferences.

There are many other built-in browser tools in addition to a multitude of third-party extensions, but this chapter has covered the basic components you'll use most frequently. I recommend you take time to explore tools to help support your task as a web developer.

Now that you know the fundamentals to jQuery and know how to utilize the browser's toolkit, you can start applying these skills with practical APEX examples. Part 2 will take a closer look at working with CSS and discuss how to use selectors within the APEX environment.

Integrating into APEX

CHAPTER 4

■ ■ ■

Enlarging Content

CSS is not only handy for dressing up applications, but it's also vital for identifying page components for triggers and actions. In Part 2, we discuss how CSS is used as a tool and how it can be integrated with APEX features, preparing you for more complicated jQuery activities.

Often when working on applications for smart devices, developers need to increase the size of components to allow for large fingers and inaccurate taps, or even just to add extra spacing within data. This chapter addresses this issue specifically and will introduce the use of browser tools in the APEX environment.

APEX Application

Now is the time to open up your APEX application and make sure it's ready, as described in the introduction. Most of the examples will be using one of two pages, a classic report or its form accompaniment. For the examples in this book, I use Oracle's ubiquitous SCOTT.EMP table, but any table that includes at least one date column should suffice.

The sample application described in the introduction has the following pages after creating a *Form on a Table with Report.*

- Page 1 – Home

- Page 2 – Employees Report

- Page 3 – Employee DML Form

The examples in this chapter increase the font size of the region title in the DML form and all the relevant fonts on the page. Finally, they enlarge the datepicker elements. These enlargements are particularly beneficial for smaller, finger-operated devices.

Enlarging the Region Title

Making the region title font isn't a big task. In fact, in APEX 5, this might be a job for template options. However, it does allow us to demonstrate all the key skills we'll be using with the browser developer tools.

Using Inspect Element to Find the Page Element

First, right click the Employee region title and choose Inspect Element. This will open the developer tools right where they are needed.

Figure 4-1 shows the region title highlighted as the cursor hovers over the `<h2>` element in APEX 4.2 using Theme 25. The Styles tab shows a font size of 12px, coming from a rule in the `4.2.css` file.

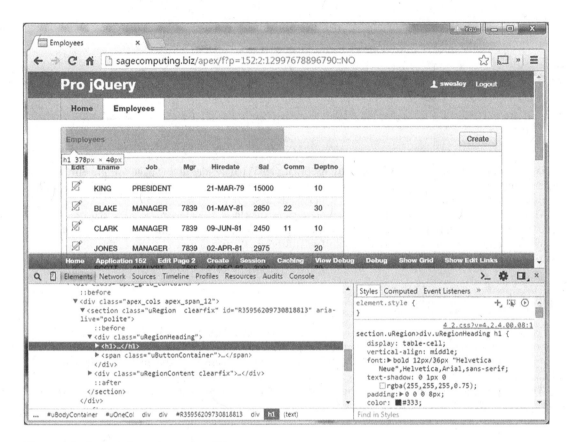

Figure 4-1. *Inspect element on region title*

Different themes found in various versions of APEX will return different results. The Universal Theme 42 in APEX 5.0 makes defining selectors slightly easier than adding classes to tags such as this, identifying it with the class `t-Region-title`.

Click the top of the Styles panel in the area with `element.style {}` to add an attribute that will overrule this size.

As Figure 4-2 shows, when you start typing "font," a list of suggestions appears. This list is very useful when looking for an attribute that will accomplish your desired task. The same drop-down appears for enumerated attribute values. Numeric values can then be scaled up or down with the arrow keys.

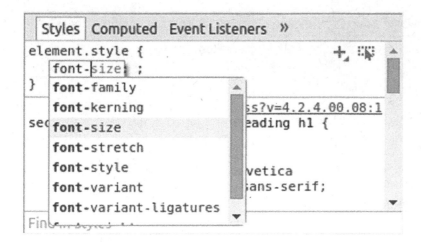

Figure 4-2. Adding custom style attribute

Increase the region title's size by setting the attribute as font-size: 150%. Note in the Elements tab the DOM has also been updated to include an inline style in the H1 element.

Turn this feature off again by unchecking the attribute in the Styles panel. Since this will only last until the page is reopened, the next step is to take note of what worked and then apply the same setting using jQuery.

Identifying CSS Selector for jQuery

This particular element was fairly easy to locate, but you need to use the tool to determine what CSS selector can be used to modify the element when using jQuery.

The bar at the bottom of the Elements panel shown in Figure 4-3 is the surrounding DOM hierarchy that represents the selected node in blue. Click the immediate <div> parent of <h1> to highlight div.uRegionHeading. This makes a great starting point for the selector as it can be used to limit which headings are identified.

Figure 4-3. Elements panel breadcrumb trail

Open the Console tab and type $('div.uRegionHeading') in the console, as shown in Figure 4-4. The browser returns any div on the page with that particular class and expands it to see everything underneath that element.

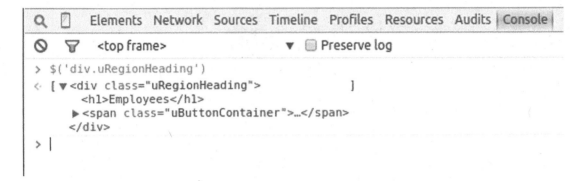

Figure 4-4. Elements panel breadcrumb trail

■ **Tip**   I recommend experimenting with these selectors as you read through this book. For instance, try it without the `.uRegionHeading` class.

---

jQuery selectors typically start with two components. The first identifies the general locale. In this case, it's a div with a certain class. Here the second becomes the identifier to be modified.

It's possible to just use h1 as the selector. However, to ensure it's only applied to titles of APEX regions, the selector becomes either

```
$('div.uRegionHeading h1')
$('div.uRegionHeading > h1')
```

The first identifies any headings underneath the specified div, while the latter states the heading must be the immediate child of the div.

The statement is extended to specify the function that applies the desired font size to H1 tags in APEX regions with this application's theme:

```
$('div.uRegionHeading h1').css('font-size','150%');
```

There is an alternative way to send styles to the `.css()` function that utilizes JSON format to define multiple attribute-value pairs. For instance, here we extend the parameter data set to include the font color red:

```
$('div.uRegionHeading h1').css({'font-size' : '150%', 'color' : 'red'});
```

More about JSON can be found in Part 3 on processes.

Using a Static Region ID

Specifying a particular region is a common task when applying jQuery. In Figure 4-3 the grandparent of h1 can be seen as #R18602627829881672. The number represents the surrogate key for the APEX metadata record for the region.

APEX allows you to specify a particular ID to be used instead, applied via the region template. Click the Employee report region and locate the Static ID field in the Advanced property group, as show in Figure 4-5.

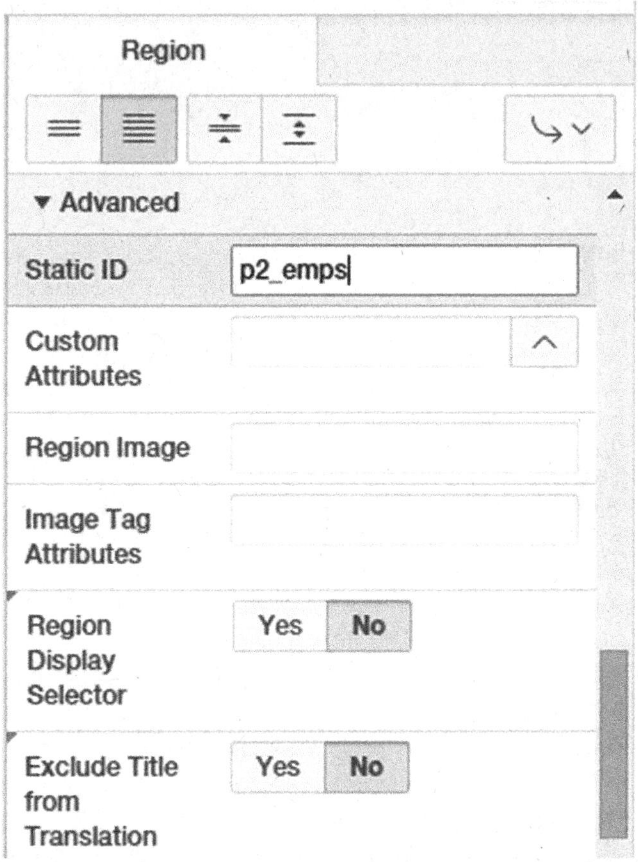

Figure 4-5. *Static ID in Region attributes*

I recommend adopting the page number style prefix with a short alias that represents the region, similar to table aliasing in SQL. Now the following selector can be used to identify headings in this particular region:

```
$('#p2_emps h1')
```

Inline CSS

Oracle developers may be aware of a general adage: If can be done in SQL, why invoke PL/SQL? Likewise, unless you want to apply formatting on demand in response to an event using JavaScript, you should use CSS.

In APEX 4.2, the development team made it easy to include CSS within your APEX pages by including specific attributes in the page properties. Edit the Page properties and scroll to the CSS section shown in Figure 4-6, with inline CSS already applied.

Figure 4-6. *Page CSS properties*

■ **Note**   Prior to APEX 4.2, you can use the APEX Developer Addon to add syntax markup to properties in the Application Builder. Visit apex.oracle.com/pls/apex/f?p=APEX_DEVELOPER_ADDON for more details.

The inline CSS shown in Figure 4-6 is the CSS equivalent of the previous jQuery statement using the JSON format. Using the inline CSS attribute will suffice while experimenting with the examples in this book. However, thanks to CSS specificity, in this case there are size and color settings that take precedence over this definition.

CSS specificity can be likened to precedence used with mathematical operators. CSS with the highest specificity is applied by the browser. Of the following two statements, the first is more specific so the font would be red, not green:

```
div.uRegionHeading h1 {color : red;}
div h1   {color : green;}
```

■ Tip Concise information on CSS specificity can be found in the W3C CSS Specification: www.w3.org/TR/CSS2/cascade.html.

While parsing a web page, the last CSS to be specified has precedence. Even if the selector used in Figure 4-6 was identical to that in 4_2.css, the inline CSS is defined in the page template first so that settings in 4_2.css are used instead. Figure 4-7 shows the inline CSS as struckthrough below the definition from the file.

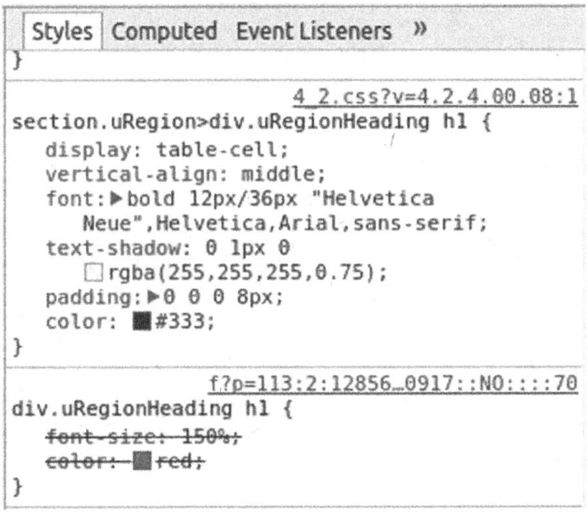

```
 Styles │ Computed  Event Listeners  »
}

                        4_2.css?v=4.2.4.00.08:1
section.uRegion>div.uRegionHeading h1 {
    display: table-cell;
    vertical-align: middle;
    font:▶bold 12px/36px "Helvetica
        Neue",Helvetica,Arial,sans-serif;
    text-shadow: 0 1px 0
        ☐rgba(255,255,255,0.75);
    padding:▶0 0 0 8px;
    color: ■#333;
}

                f.?p=113:2:12856…0917::NO:::70
div.uRegionHeading h1 {
    font-size: 150%;
    color:■red;
}
```

Figure 4-7. Style precedence

The sledgehammer approach to overcoming this is to include the !important tag, as per Listing 4-1, but this is not generally accepted as good practice. Defining CSS in the application's custom .css file overcomes some specificity issues and adds other advantages. It helps maintenance, modularization, and performance—the same reasons that PL/SQL should be specified in packages, limiting inline use.

Listing 4-1. Inline CSS for the Employee Report Page

```
div.uRegionHeading h1 {
    font-size : 150% !important;
    color : red !important;
}
```

There are identical jQuery and CSS properties at the page template level so you can apply these settings once to influence multiple pages, though the ideal scenario is to ultimately put your CSS in a .css file and include the file in the "File URLs."

Increase Font Sizes throughout the Page

Web pages for a tablet-sized device would have different types of elements that need font-size increases. Only a few selectors could identify the majority of those elements. Input fields also require the line height attribute to be increased to accommodate the larger text.

Prior to APEX 5.0, CSS such as that shown in Listing 4-2 would be added to the application's CSS library to cover the majority of components displayed on a page. With the advent of APEX 5.0, this is now accomplished with ease using declarative Template Options.

Listing 4-2. Enlarging All Font Sizes

```
/* input items */
#uBodyContainer input{
  font-size:120%;
  line-height: 130%;
}
#modal_width input{
  font-size:140%;
  line-height: 130%;
}

#uBodyContainer textarea
,#modal_width textarea{
  font-size: 130%;
  line-height: 130%;
}

/* labels */
a.uHelpLink
,label.uRequired
,label.uOptional
,select.selectlist
,span.display_only
,fieldset.radio_group label
{
  font-size:130% !important;
}
```

Enlarging Datepicker Elements

Datepickers were the first widgets targeted for enlargement while navigating through a prototype application for a tablet application. The individual dates were simply too small for large fingers to accurately touch, and there is no granular Template Option specific to datepickers.

Figure 4-8. *Original APEX 5.0 datepicker size*

Figure 4-8 shows the datepicker in its original format. The first step is to increase the font size for components within the datepicker, though the exact selector varies across themes:

```
body .ui-datepicker table {
  font-size:200%;
}
```

As Figure 4-9 illustrates, increasing the font size is not enough. The CSS padding around each table cell that represents a date also needs to be increased. Otherwise, the individual dates will still be difficult to tap with a finger.

Figure 4-9. *Datepicker with increased font size*

Figure 4-10 is the final product with all date cells padded. APEX 5.0 needed special treatment to match datepicker width to padded cells using the following code:

```
/* Cell padding */
body .ui-datepicker td a.ui-state-default {
  padding:12px;
}
/* Picker width */
body .ui-datepicker {
  width: 406px;
}
```

◄		March 1979				►
Su	Mo	Tu	We	Th	Fr	Sa
				1	2	3
4	5	6	7	8	9	10
11	12	13	14	15	16	17
18	19	20	21	22	23	24
25	26	27	28	29	30	31

Figure 4-10. *Datepicker with cell padding*

Listing 4-3 is the complete listing for the Inline CSS page property in the Employee form.

Listing 4-3. Attributes to Enlarge Datepicker Components

```
/* Font size */
body .ui-datepicker table {
  font-size:200%;
}
/* Cell padding */
body .ui-datepicker td a.ui-state-default {
  padding:12px;
}
/* Picker width */
body .ui-datepicker {
  width: 406px;
}
```

Increase the size of the datepicker icon would be a separate task, tackled using the datepicker icon attributes in the Theme properties.

Summary

While this chapter focused on using CSS commands to enlarge page content, it also demonstrated vital techniques for using the browser tools to help identify page components to be manipulated. These tools also allow testing of attribute settings that will ultimately be incorporated into the APEX code base.

The location of the code is important, not just for CSS selectivity but future re-use and performance. More CSS selectors were also explored and the use of a static region ID will be particularly useful for jQuery techniques.

Selectors will also vary across APEX themes, but the browser tools work consistently to help you identify the selector relevant to your theme. Most of the time, it's a slight variation in class name.

CHAPTER 5

■ ■ ■

Firing Dynamic Actions

Dynamic actions are a marquee APEX 4.x feature readers should be aware of. In fact, if you've ever used a dynamic action, you've already used some jQuery on your page, albeit declaratively. Understanding the different options to invoke them is a key step to the use of CSS and jQuery.

This chapter demonstrates dynamic actions and relates them to the world of jQuery. We will provide further insight into how to operate jQuery alternatives in Chapter 6.

The chapter's example extends a classic report to include a Google-like auto filter. It then explores two options for invoking a context-sensitive dynamic action when clicking a link for a particular row.

Creating a New Report Page

The example created in this chapter won't open the form page; it will just demonstrate how dynamic actions can interact with an APEX page. For this reason, you should create a separate classic report page and leave the existing report/form combination alone.

To begin, create a new classic report page on the EMP table (your own table is fine). As a shortcut, ensure you set the Enable Search option as shown in Figure 5-1.

Figure 5-1. *Classic report attribute settings in creation wizard*

Refresh Report on Search

Many people may have experiences with web sites that automatically refresh data as they type. It's possible to react to user typing with a dynamic action listening for change of the field. The action reacts by triggering a partial page refresh of just the report.

Search Field Listener

First, create a dynamic action to listen for any key presses in the search field. This will trigger a refresh of the report. The dynamic action event will be on Key Release and the selection type on the search field page item, as shown in Figure 5-2.

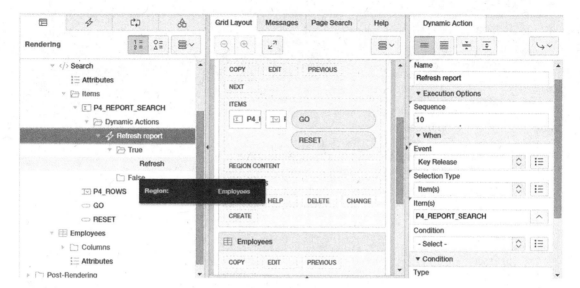

Figure 5-2. *Dynamic action to refresh report on key releasev*

Submit page item

When the employee region is refreshed, the database needs to be aware of the updated value in the search field within the browsers so that correct results can be returned. This is done by either a separate PL/SQL action prior to the refresh or modifying the Page Item To Submit attribute in the region definition to include the relevant page item, as seen in Figure 5-3.

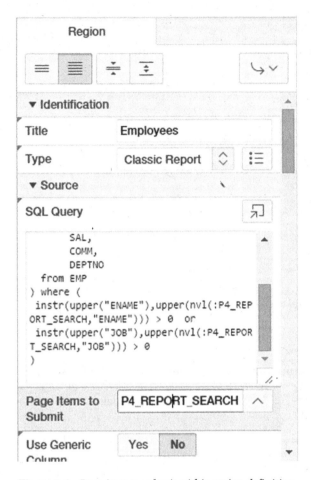

Figure 5-3. *Page item to submit within region definition*

Now run the page and start typing in the search field. The report will automatically refresh, highlighting the characters typed within the report (if you used the "enable search" wizard option).

■ **Note**   If the report still doesn't refresh, check the report attributes setting `Enable Partial Page Refresh` is set to Yes.

Responding to Row Click

In the original report/form combination, clicking the employee number would open the record in the APEX form on another page. It's possible to define dynamic actions that also respond to a click (or a tap), which could then perform alternative actions rather than opening a page, such as opening a modal dialog.

There are two decent options when defining the dynamic actions. Both allow further information to be gathered about which record was clicked, and both introduce a few more jQuery concepts.

Option A: Invoke Custom Event

Invoking a custom event can be likened to calling a process on demand. This option modifies the link attributes to call a dynamic action directly.

First, change the EMPNO report column type to Link. Then set the column link properties, as per Figure 5-4. Not yet available to the screenshot is the Link Text of #EMPNO#, prompted for once the target is defined.

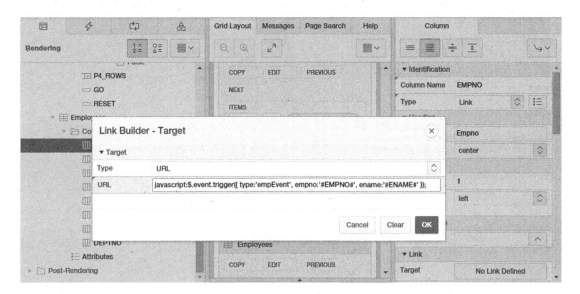

Figure 5-4. *Link properties for empno column*

Edit link definition

The URL target is actually a JavaScript call to a function in the apex.event namespace. The JavaScript namespace can be likened to a PL/SQL package since they're both a collection of modules. This function is made to invoke a dynamic action referencing the event empEvent.

```
javascript:$.event.trigger({ type:'empEvent', empno:'#EMPNO#', ename:'#ENAME#' });
```

The ability to pass further information about the record can be advantageous, particularly with modal pop ups. A more basic call passing just one parameter can be defined as the following:

```
javascript:$.event.trigger('empEvent','#EMPNO#');
```

Define Dynamic Action

Now define a new dynamic action that defines the custom event invoked by the report anchor, as shown in Figure 5-5. This dynamic action doesn't use a pre-defined event, but is the definition of the custom event invoked on demand when the user clicks a row.

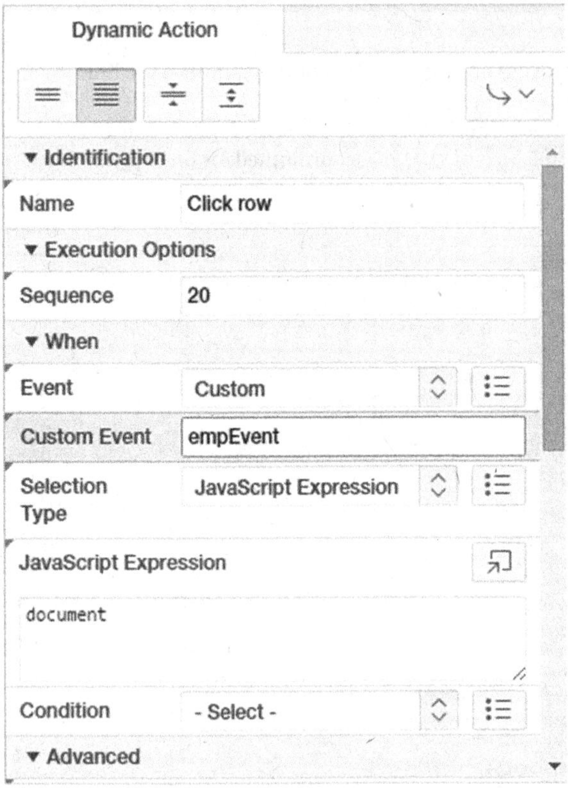

Figure 5-5. *Dynamic action definition for custom event*

The Custom Event name matches the type used when invoking JavaScript. In APEX 4.x, the Selection Type was DOM Object, with the DOM Object attribute as "document".

The responding action can reference information from the click event using `this.browserEvent` object. Defined as a JavaScript action, it could output to the console the parameter values using this snippet:

```
console.log(this.browserEvent.empno);
console.log(this.browserEvent.ename);
```

Single parameter calls need only refer to `this.data`. Further information is available in the help text accompanying the JavaScript Code attribute, shown in Figure 5-6. Any information about the row can be sent to a process or be applied to a page item, depending on the page's needs.

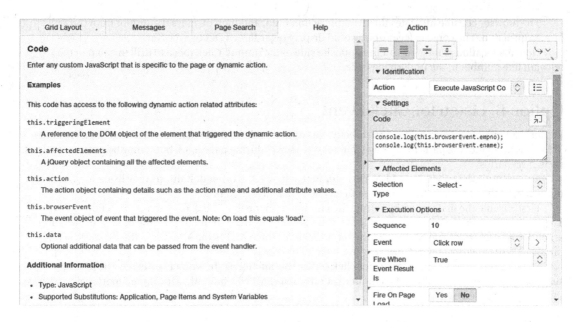

Figure 5-6. *Custom dynamic action JavaScript event, with associated help*

Rather than invoking a dynamic action directly, this option adds an event listener to certain page elements. This adds more moving parts to the page and may be slower during page load, but it may be more suitable in certain scenarios. Figure 5-7 shows the page at runtime in debug mode, with the browser console open after clicking on an Empno link.

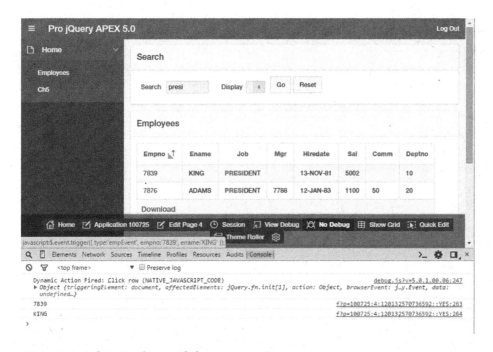

Figure 5-7. *Debugging the row click event at runtime*

The browser console indicates the dynamic action fired, and then displays the output from the JavaScript action. The console log output would display regardless if Debug were on.

Note the location of the code on the opposite side of the output. Click these to drill through to the relevant line number in the underlying code.

Option B: Listen for Click Event

Rather than invoking a dynamic action directly, this option adds an event listener to certain page elements. This adds more moving parts to the page and may be slower during page load, but it may be more suitable in certain scenarios.

The example described here adds a listener for each row, but other definitions may listen for a click on the region itself, and then work out if the object clicked has a related task.

First, disable the first option by setting the condition on the first "Click row" dynamic action to Never. The Empno link now only needs to call javascript:void(0);, but it won't impact the outcome if you don't amend it. Add a Static ID of p4_emps to the report region, which makes the selector in the dynamic action more efficient by adding the region ID as the search boundary.

Create a dynamic action listening for click on the row anchor as shown in Figure 5-8. The jQuery selector isolates anchor (link) in the column with the alias EMPNO, but only within the report region with the id report_p4_emps.

```
#report_p4_emps td[headers="EMPNO"] a
```

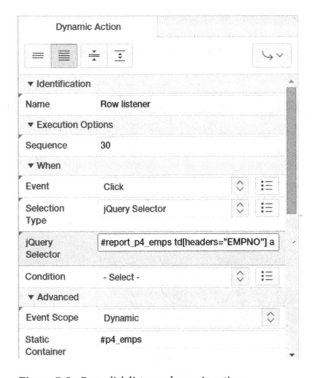

Figure 5-8. *Row click listener dynamic action*

Note this dynamic action uses a dynamic event scope. This means the listeners are reapplied upon refresh of the region, such as when the user restricts records within a search. The static container specifies tighter scope for the browser to search for matching selectors.

The JavaScript action in Figure 5-9 uses another dynamic action related attribute this.triggeringElement. In this case, it returns the anchor, so further information about the row can be garnered when used as a jQuery selector by traversing the DOM hierarchy.

```
console.log($(this.triggeringElement).text());
```

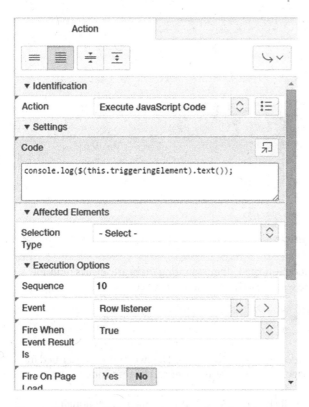

Figure 5-9. *Row click dynamic action JavaScript event*

Figure 5-10 shows the runtime page with this dynamic action responding to the event.

51

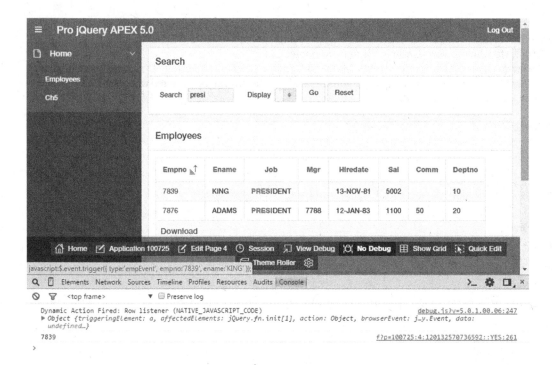

Figure 5-10. *Debugging the row listener event at runtime*

Once again, the browser delivers the information requested, demonstrating there are always multiple ways to solve problems with the toolkit at hand. One was proactive, the other reactive.

Summary

Dynamic actions are closely coupled with jQuery selectors and tree traversal. The two options described in this chapter illustrate the basic mechanics of how page interaction by the user can be responded to by the APEX application.

Dynamic actions give APEX developers plenty of declarative tools. Writing the same functionality yourself using only jQuery can provide added flexibility.

CHAPTER 6

■ ■ ■

Implementing jQuery Alternatives

This chapter presents the final step on integrating jQuery into the APEX environment. In this chapter, we will recreate the declarative examples from the previous chapter using jQuery.

Some may consider this process extra legwork, but with custom jQuery comes other advantages—it comes down to finding a balance. More complex dynamic actions tend to read better as jQuery code.

Utilizing jQuery within APEX also brings other requirements and responsibilities, so this chapter will aim to prepare you for the examples in the remainder of the book.

jQuery in APEX

In Chapter 4, I mentioned differences between using inline CSS and using external files to define styling. JavaScript and jQuery face similar issues, some you would already be familiar with as a PL/SQL developer.

Why Not Use Dynamic Actions?

When building APEX applications, you don't just use the wizards—the same can be said for dynamic actions and JavaScript. Dynamic actions are great for simple tasks and learning capabilities; however, manually written JavaScript can provide some benefits comparable to PL/SQL packages.

Finding the right balance is key, and a client of mine follows a mantra I agree with: "Complexity always goes somewhere." Dynamic actions are declarative and integrated within other product features, but extensive use means many actions with code spaghettified throughout your page.

JavaScript contained within one file can provide modularization with function calls and flexibility with conditional processing, but it requires a higher level of expertise. One size does not fit all cases, and it takes time to find the balance for each project.

Where Do I Put My jQuery Code?

While experimenting with the examples in this book, place jQuery in either the Function and Global Variable Declaration or Execute when Page Loads attribute in page properties, as shown in Figure 6-1.

Figure 6-1. JavaScript attributes in APEX Page properties

For larger projects, you should place jQuery within suitably modular .js files, just like you modularize PL/SQL procedures in database packages. These supporting files would be included using the File URLs attribute, at page, template, or User Interface level.

Since you may need to reference a number of files from the same location, you can define the JavaScript file location within a substitution string in the application definition, and then refer to the location using substitution string syntax. For example:

```
&JS_LOCATION.myapp_p5.css
```

Resources

I highly recommend familiarizing yourself with the Oracle Application Express API Reference, linked from the main documentation page for your APEX version. Utilization of JavaScript within the APEX environment is growing fast and the JavaScript APIs in particular are a good point of reference.

There are a number of APEX bloggers who are particularly generous with their posts on jQuery functionality. Searching "jQuery" in the APEX blog aggregator at www.odtug.com/apex will return dozens of results.

Instrumentation

The simplest form of instrumentation within JavaScript is the console.log() function, whose use is similar to dbms_output.put_line(). It's not supported by all browsers and calls shouldn't remain in production code. A better alternative is to use apex.debug(). It's a wrapper provided by APEX that will output information to the console only when in debug mode.

The most comprehensive option is Logger, an instrumentation utility originally written for PL/SQL by Tyler Muth, but extended specifically for APEX and JavaScript by Martin Giffy D'Souza. The library can be found at www.oraopensource.com/logger, a trustworthy open source project for Oracle products.

Whatever option you choose, I urge you to take instrumentation seriously and log function calls, parameters, and key events. Doing so will make future debugging much simpler, and that debugger is often your future self.

Naming Conventions

I've already suggested referring to the page number in the static region ID. I also recommend referring to the page number when defining functions used as jQuery callbacks, particularly since many of them will be specific to a particular page.

I tend to adopt coding convention in JavaScript that mirrors what I do in PL/SQL. This may ruffle feathers of JavaScript purists and my APEX colleagues, but in the APEX world I find it provides normalcy and consistency. Set standards that suit your team and apply them.

jQuery Style Key Release

Create a new page as a copy of the previous chapter, and then remove the three dynamic actions. Edit the page properties and add Listing 6-1 to the Execute when Page Loads attribute.

■ **Caution** When utilizing code listings, always ensure the page numbers match up with the page numbers in your application.

Listing 6-1. Refresh Region on Search

```
// refresh list on search
$('#P6_REPORT_SEARCH').keyup(
  function(evt) {

    // simple return of HTML ID that caused event
    console.log(evt.target.id);

    // jQuery wraps this DOM element to get info
    console.log('Value:'+$(this).val()); // item value

    // evt is equivalent to this.browserEvent in DA
    console.log('key:'+evt.keyCode); // which key pressed?

    // refresh report region
    $('#p6_emps').trigger('apexrefresh');
  }
);
```

The selector identifies the search item, and the .keyup() function is the same used by the key release dynamic action event. The function accepts an event object that can be interrogated to obtain information about the page component related to the event.

The only requirement of this function is to trigger a refresh of the classic report region that supports a partial page refresh. Therefore, the search field now has an extra listener applied on page load that can be verifiedwithin the browser tools. Inspect the search item and view the event listeners as shown in Figure 6-2.

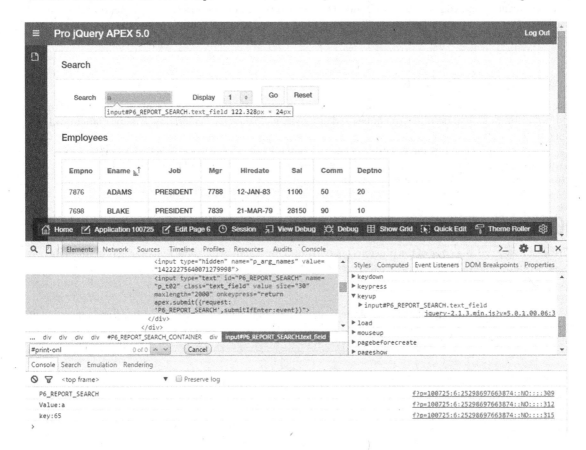

Figure 6-2. *Browser tools indicating event listeners on an item, including results in console log*

The keyup event has now been added to the list of event listeners for the input item. Also note the onkeypress attribute, honouring an item attribute set to submit when enter pressed. The three units of information in the console output represent key data that can influence logic typically placed throughout the page. Further information can be found in the event and item objects and you'll encounter more examples through the book.

Report Link Event Listener

In Chapter 5, Option A executes JavaScript directly and doesn't need a manual alternative. Option B adds a listener to page elements and is a good candidate for demonstrating the manual alternative.

Simplify Anchor URL

The anchor doesn't need to perform an active operation and can be modified to a call similar to the null; PL/SQL operation, or NOOP in the assembly world. Edit the EMPNO link column to modify the column link URL to the following:

```
javascript:void(0);
```

Now clicking on the anchor does nothing, so another component is required to listen for such an event.

Define Row Click Listener

The listener for the report row anchor is analogous to the declarative dynamic action. The selector for the anchor is supplied so some JavaScript can be called when the user clicks the anchor.

Extend the Execute when Page Loads attribute with code from Listing 6-2. This adds an on click listener for anchors within the EMPNO column in the region.

Listing 6-2. Event Listener for Report Anchor

```
// on click of anchor
$('#p6_emps').on('click'    // region
  ,'td[headers="EMPNO"] a'  // element in region
  ,function(evt) {
    // $(this) = $(evt.target)
    console.log('html:'+$(this).text());
  }
);
```

The selector to the function only includes the region name, where the selector to the specific anchor is supplied as the second parameter. This allows the listener to still work after a partial page refresh of the region. If the entire selector were supplied, then the listener would need to be reapplied after refresh. Similar functionality is applied by setting the Event Scope attribute in dynamic actions to Dynamic.

■ **Note**   The .on() function has had incarnations in previous versions of jQuery as .bind(), live(), and .delegate().

Summary

Dynamic actions are closely coupled with jQuery selectors and tree traversal. The two options described in this chapter illustrate the basic mechanics of how page interaction by the user can be responded to by the APEX application.

Dynamic actions give APEX developers plenty of declarative tools. However, writing the same functionality yourself using only jQuery can provide added flexibility and re-use options. Common solution patterns end up being written as library functions in your growing JavaScript repertoire, which is difficult to replicate when defined solely as dynamic actions.

CHAPTER 7

■ ■ ■

Highlighting Selected Row

So far in the book I have covered the underlying principles behind utilizing jQuery within the Oracle APEX environment and how CSS is closely integrated with how jQuery works, but we have yet to demonstrate truly applicable examples.

Highlighting a row within a classic report after the row is clicked will bring together some fundamental lessons learned so far, showing techniques that will be further expanded upon throughout the remainder of the book.

This chapter introduces a development pattern that you will be able to apply to your own applications and, as a result, not rely on copying code from the book.

jQuery Development Pattern

The key steps required to highlight a row illustrate the typical workflow required for many jQuery examples:

1. Use the inspect element tool to locate the jQuery selector and test styling

2. Define the CSS that will serve the highlighted row

3. Define a jQuery function that will apply the highlight

4. Add an even listener that will execute the function

5. *Traverse* the DOM to remove existing highlighting, while using *chaining* to improve performance

Practice each of these steps and you will be able to apply different combinations to solve different types of problems. In this case, apply the highlight to your original classic report page.

Using Inspect Element

In Chapter 3, I described how to use the Inspect Element browser tool, a ubiquitous feature in web development.

First, run the original employee report page and right click one of the employee records. Then select *Inspect Element* to show the DOM in the Elements panel of the browser tools. To make things interesting, be sure to select an even-numbered row (with the non-white background).

It's likely the browser will highlight a specific <td> cell in the report. Select the parent <tr> as shown in Figure 7-1 since this is what needs to be highlighted.

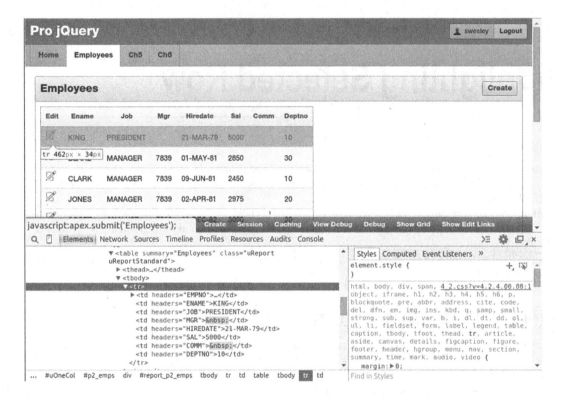

Figure 7-1. *Inspect row properties of classic report*

In the Styles panel, add a background colour to the row (in between the element.style brackets):

```
background-color: red;
```

On even-numbered rows, this will have no effect because the standard APEX report region alternates the row color at cell level, which means it has a higher CSS specificity, even with the !important rule.

Odd-numbered rows have no such attribute so a row-level background color will affect the output, but only when the mouse is not hovering in the row. Therefore, the row highlight will need to be applied at the cell level.

A selector for cells within the report can be determined using the DOM breadcrumb trail at the bottom of Figure 7-1. A few variations would be acceptable depending on what's displayed on the page, though readability and performance can vary.

The ideal selector often utilizes classes to be specific about which elements to include or exclude. Without them, you may unwittingly include the header row or pagination elements:

```
# p2_emps table. t-Report-report tr td
```

The .t-Report-report class wasn't directly specified in the breadcrumb trail, but the attribute can be seen in the parent table tag in Figure 7-1. Clicking the table node will list any classes for that tag in the breadcrumb trail.

> ■ **Note**   The table's class may vary if you haven't used Theme 42. Themes 25 and 26 use uReport, even older themes use theme number as prefix.

Not specifying enough components in the selector may also mean not enough nodes are snipped from the DOM. For instance, excluding the report ID will mean tables with that class from other regions will also be returned.

Defining the CSS

The selector currently locates all relevant cells within the specified report region. To transform this into CSS that will conditionally apply a highlight, a new class needs to be conjured.

Listing 7-1 extends the selector to reference the class rowHighlightClassic. Only rows with this class will be highlighted, and the click event will apply this class to the relevant row. Apply this listing to the page's Inline CSS attribute.

Listing 7-1. Row Highlight for Classic Reports

```
// clicked row
body table.t-Report-report tr.rowHighlightClassic td {
   background-color: #FFFFCC !important;
}
// overwrite existing definitions for hover
.t-Report--rowHighlight .t-Report-report tr:hover .t-Report-cell
,.t-Report--rowHighlight .t-Report-report tr:nth-child(odd):hover .t-Report-cell{
   background-color: #FFFF99 !important;
}
```

Also note the specific region ID has been replaced with the body tag. This means the styling is suitable for any report regions in the application.

The second selector includes the :hover keyword, displaying a slightly different shade when the mouse hovers over a row that has been highlighted. The specified colors are two light shades of yellow.

The !important rule ensures any localized highlighting is overwritten. The use of this rule is often frowned upon as it can be highly abused, but it's a fair implementation in this particular case. You can avoid usage by adjusting selectors to match existing specificity.

Adding the Event Listener

The legwork has already been done in regard to the selector required for the listener on click of a row, I've just removed the td from the end. When executed on load, the following code will add the rowHighlightClassic class to the row clicked in the p2_emp report:

```
$('#p2_emps').on('click', 'table.t-Report-report tbody tr', function(index) {
   $(this).addClass("rowHighlightClassic");
});
```

What it doesn't do is remove any existing highlights that may have been applied. More code needs to be added to the callback section to complete the requirements.

Note the code could have been written without the optional selector parameter, but the listener would not be present after a refresh of the region unless the listeners were reapplied after refresh:

```
$('#p2_emps table.t-Report-report tbody tr').on('click', function(index) {
    $(this).addClass("rowHighlightClassic");
});
```

Figure 7-2 shows the page where multiple rows have been clicked, hence containing the rowHighlightClassic class. The Styles panel indicates the yellow background color over overwriting that was found in the supplied Vita.min.css file, thanks to the !important rule.

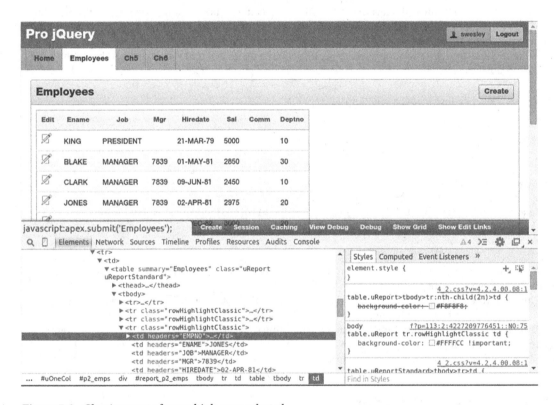

Figure 7-2. *Classic report after multiple rows selected*

Define the Highlight Function

At this point, it's worth defining the function separately so as not to embed too much code within the listener definition. It also makes for good modularization as the function can be parameterized and used by other pages.

You'll find the function definition in Listing 7-2 comparable to a PL/SQL procedure. It accepts a loosely typed parameter that, in this case, is jQuery object for the selected table row, referenced using this in the listener callback.

Listing 7-2. Generic Highlight Row Function for Classic Reports

```
function highlightRowClassic(pElement){
    // remove highlight from other row
    $(pElement)
      .closest('tbody')                        // upto body
      .children('tr.rowHighlightClassic')  // find row with class
      .removeClass("rowHighlightClassic"); // remove class

    // make sure done before adding new highlight
    $(pElement).addClass("rowHighlightClassic");
}
```

The function traverses up the DOM to first find the closest tbody tag above the row that was clicked. It then locates all previously highlighted rows under that node using the .children() function.

Previously highlighted rows are identified with the class on the table row, which are subsequently removed by the .removeClass function.

All function calls are chained and can be read chronologically from left to right. This allows jQuery to apply these steps in one movement, hence improving performance.

Clearing existing highlighting is done before adding the highlight to the selected row using the .addClass() function and using the selector supplied in the parameter.

Add Listing 7-2 to the *Function and Global Declaration* page attribute, and then modify the listener to replace the .addClass() function with the following call. The JavaScript attributes in the page definition should match Figure 7-3.

```
highlightRowClassic(this);
```

Function and Global Variable Declaration

```
1  function highlightRowClassic(pElement){
2      // remove highlight from other row, make sure done before new highlight
3      $(pElement).closest('tbody').children('tr.rowHighlightClassic').removeClass("rowHighlightClassic");
4      $(pElement).addClass("rowHighlightClassic");
5  }
```

Editor Setting: Textarea - HTML/XML - **Javascript** - PL/SQL

Execute when Page Loads

```
1  $('#report_p2_emps table.uReport tbody tr').on('click', function(index) {
2      //$(this).addClass("rowHighlightClassic");
3      highlightRowClassic(this);
4  });
```

Figure 7-3. JavaScript page settings to highlight selected row

Now refresh the report page and click different rows. The last row clicked will be the only row highlighted.

Summary

This chapter has applied the basic steps required to investigate the elements of an APEX page before defining appropriate CSS, and then leveraging information already garnered to define the required jQuery to perform an action on the page in response to an event.

The individual steps required to complete this action will be useful in future chapters as needs vary and the examples become more complex.

Subsequent chapters will use a similar format to guide you through more practical examples that you can apply in your own applications.

■ ■ ■

Adding Buttons to Reports

A common requirement in some form or another is to respond to a click somewhere on a particular record. Mobile applications in particular respond better with buttons than old-fashioned anchor links.

Typically, a mouse click or finger tap would invoke some process that either manipulates the page or communicates with the database. This chapter demonstrates the common framework required to facilitate such a requirement and explores options to get information about the row.

In Chapter 9, we begin to explore the processes underneath these buttons and behaviors.

Defining the Button

There will always be a number of ways to style a button on the page. You can replicate the APEX button templates, source specific CSS from the Web, define your own CSS, use an example from another application, or simply use the HTML button tag.

The style used may also vary over time. In the past, the multidimensional skeuomorphic design was popular, while contemporary web sites use a flattened user interface. The example in this chapter demonstrates how you can replicate functionality from an existing packaged APEX application.

Deriving the Button Style

While exploring the APEX-packaged applications, I found that some (such as the Sample Database Application) had buttons in reports that I wanted to replicate.

Using the inspect element tool in Figure 8-1, you can find button styling properties necessary to replicate the button in your own application.

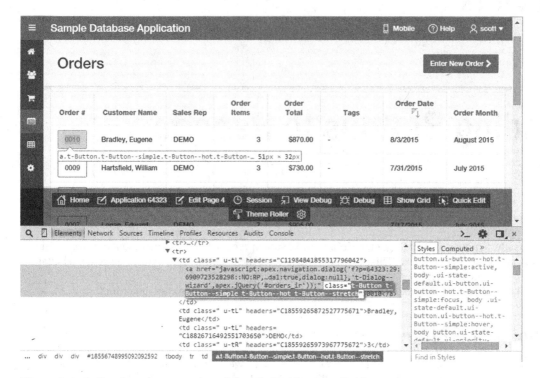

Figure 8-1. *Styling from the pre-packaged Sample Database Application*

Just the classes are required when using the same theme. Otherwise, properties would need to be harvested from the Styles panel. In this case, the following classes will be copied:

```
t-Button t-Button--simple t-Button--hot
```

Generating the Button

In this case, the classes simply need to be added to a link defined in a Universal Themed report. Leave the existing link to open the Employee Form and, instead, add another column to expand upon later.

Add a virtual column to the Employees report by right clicking within the report columns in the tree pane, as shown in Figure 8-2. Virtual columns are available in 4.x in the right-hand task menu when editing report attributes.

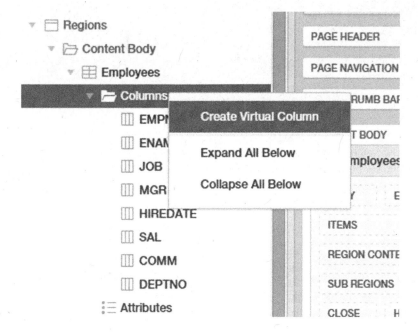

Figure 8-2. *Create virtual column in Page Designer*

The link definition defines the details for the button, as shown in Figure 8-3. The link text will be the button label, so the #EMPNO# substitution string is used to include report data as the label. The link attributes are used to add the desired button classes to the generated anchor:

```
class="t-Button t-Button--simple t-Button--hot"
```

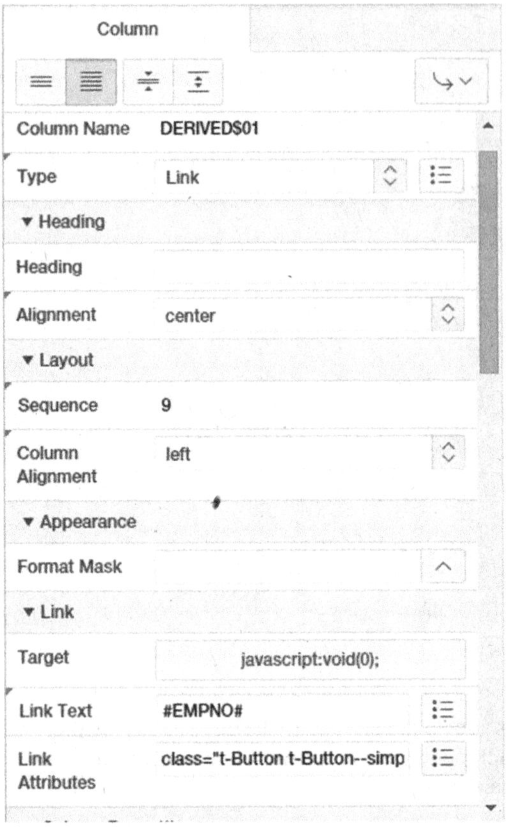

Figure 8-3. *Column link definition for the button*

Note all code referenced in this chapter is found in Listing 8-1 in the source code available online.

While invoking a custom event as described in Chapter 5 is the simplest way to pass a discrete amount of information to the handler, I want to show how you can garner information directly from the row definition using jQuery.

Specify `javascript:void(0);` as the link target to ensure the link does nothing on click. This is JavaScript's version of a `NOOP` or `null;` operation. Instead, we'll define a dynamic action to listen for click events on the report buttons.

Preparing the Dynamic Action

Define a click dynamic action on the Employees page, listening for click on the report buttons using the following jQuery selector:

```
#p2_emps a.t-Button
```

The rest of this chapter details options for the relevant action. For now, set it to run JavaScript that outputs the triggering element using the following:

```
console.log(this.triggeringElement);
```

The runtime report will now look like Figure 8-4, with the result of a button click in the browser console.

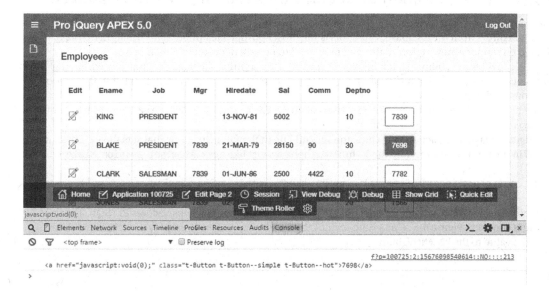

Figure 8-4. *Classic report with buttons*

Gathering Information about the Row

Information about the row can be used to make decisions about what actions are made available to the user. A number of options are available for gathering further information about the row, and there are pros and cons across all options.

The option utilized will depend on your requirement. The major difference relates to how up-to-date the information needs to be. Some options utilize information that's derived while rendering the page, saving round trips to the database to gather more information about the row being acted upon.

Other situations require more dynamic access to related information. This could mean determining the value from input items in a tabular form, or invoking a process to fetch fresh information from the database.

Sending Discrete Values

Option A from Chapter 5 described how to use a custom event to pass information to the dynamic action using a link definition such as

```
javascript:$.event.trigger('DAEvent', [['#EMPNO#','#ENAME#']]);
```

This option minimizes the amount of work required by the browser, but it is more suitable for a small number values formulated during render of the page.

This option sends information from the anchor, while the other options described in this chapter obtain all information from within the invoked dynamic action.

Using a Dynamic Action to Get Live Information from the Database

Discrete information such as the row's primary key can be used as input to a PL/SQL action, obtaining live information direct from the database. Often this is the most appropriate option as information on the page generated on render is now stale and the user may need to make a decision based on live data.

APEX provides the ability to fetch information without submitting the page declaratively within the dynamic action. More detailed information on called processes can be found in Chapter 9, but this section shows how the dynamic action can operate.

Create two text items in the employee region called P2_EMPNO and P2_ENAME. Leave them as text items so you can see how and when they're populated.

Extend the JavaScript action to include the second line in the following code that sets the P2_EMPNO item to the ID in the button clicked: Note the $s function behaves just like apex_item.set_session_state.

```
console.log(this.triggeringElement); $s('P2_EMPNO',$(this.triggeringElement).text());
```

Now define a second action that executes after the JavaScript, but this one executes PL/SQL. The final outcome is shown in Figure 8-5. This action fetches the current name for the employee clicked and then returns the value to the P2_ENAME item.

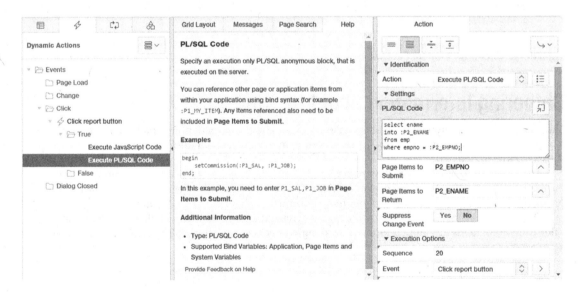

Figure 8-5. *PL/SQL action that talks to the database from the browser*

The browser is now aware what record was clicked thanks to $s() function setting P2_EMPNO. This information is passed from the browser to the database thanks to the Page Items to Submit property. This allows the PL/SQL to reference the value of the item set in the browser.

If the PL/SQL action updates session state for any page items, these values can be reflected in the browser by specifying relevant fields in the Page Items to Return property.

Note when designing your UI that repeated trips to the database can decrease performance of the application and introduce lag to the user, particularly on mobile networks where coverage is poor.

Dynamic Action Attributes

The JavaScript action in the dynamic action for the button click has access to a number of attributes made available specifically for dynamic actions. Further information on such properties can be found by clicking the Help tab in the middle pane of the Page Designer and placing the cursor in the relevant property field. Clicking the JavaScript Code attribute will show the popup in Figure 8-6.

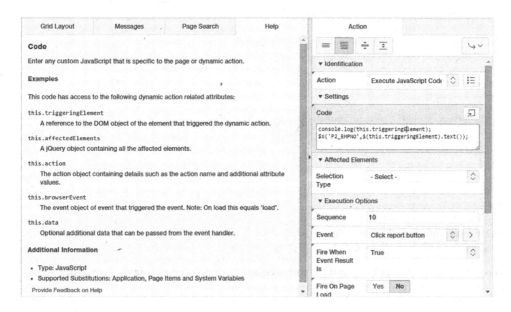

Figure 8-6. *Attribute help for the Code attribute in JavaScript actions*

For the dynamic action on the report anchor, this.triggeringElement returned the anchor object for the row clicked. Since this is a DOM object, surrounding it with the jQuery $() function allowed interrogation of the textual content, hence the EMPNO value:

```
<a href="javascript:void(0);" class="t-Button t-Button--simple t-Button--hot">7698</a>
```

Utilizing dynamic action attributes are fundamental to the following options.

71

Traversing the Tree for Information

Clicking the button in the row may require obtaining information from other columns in the row, particularly within tabular forms where the user may have modified the data.

Since this.triggeringElement returns the DOM object for the anchor, it's possible to laterally traverse the tree to return information from other columns.

For instance, to determine the salary of the relevant employee clicked chain, the following jQuery functions together from the triggering element:

```
$(this.triggeringElement).closest('tr').find('td[headers="SAL"]').text()
```

The call climbs the tree to the closest table row, then locates the column with header property equal to SAL, and, finally, returns the text shown in that column. Figure 8-7 shows the related DOM where the jQuery would start at the button anchor, climb to the tr element, and then return the figure 5002 from the SAL column.

```
▼ <table class="t-Report-report" summary="Employees">
  ▶ <thead>...</thead>
  ▼ <tbody>
    ▼ <tr>
      ▶ <td class="t-Report-cell" headers="EMPNO">...</td>
        <td class="t-Report-cell" headers="ENAME">KING</td>
        <td class="t-Report-cell" headers="JOB">PRESIDENT</td>
        <td class="t-Report-cell" headers="MGR"> </td>
        <td class="t-Report-cell" headers="HIREDATE">13-NOV-81</td>
        <td class="t-Report-cell" headers="SAL">5002</td>
        <td class="t-Report-cell" headers="COMM"> </td>
        <td class="t-Report-cell" headers="DEPTNO">10</td>
      ▼ <td class="t-Report-cell" headers="DERIVED$01">
          <a href="javascript:void(0);" class="t-Button t-Button--simple t-Button--hot">7839</a>
        </td>
      </tr>
    ▶ <tr class>...</tr>
```

Figure 8-7. DOM representation of a row in the report

This method makes any information about the row accessible using the appropriate traversal functions and selectors.

Using Data Attributes

Not all required information about a row may be displayed to the user, nor do you need to define them as hidden items within the report, but you don't want to make a round trip to the database. HTML5 provides the ability to define your own custom attributes to tags with data-* attributes. Modify the button's Link Attributes to include the following:

```
data-ename="#ENAME#"
```

Doing so will extend the generated DOM to include data relevant for the row. For example:

```
<a href="javascript:void(0)" class="t-Button t-Button--simple t-Button--hot"
data-ename="KING">
```

These data attributes can be interrogated from the dynamic action using the `.data()` function, accepting the suffix of the attribute as the parameter:

```
$(this.triggeringElement).data('ename');
```

This provides a lightweight method of including extra information about the row while the page is generated, ready for instant access by JavaScript events instead of fetching fresh information across the network from the database.

Summary

Adding buttons to reports is the one option to provide added functionality to users. This chapter has provided a number of options to get information about the row clicked so the action button can make the right decisions.

Selecting which option to use will depend on the requirements of the application and expectations of the users, but APEX and jQuery combine to provide the flexibility to solve whatever scenario you encounter.

Playing with Processes

CHAPTER 9

■ ■ ■

Choosing Process Options

The time has come to investigate methods of communicating with the database without submitting the page. Such techniques enable the developer to craft more responsive and user-friendly applications by giving the user context-sensitive feedback and the ability to save information in response to a page event.

This chapter looks at the differences between four major alternatives to help you decide which one might be appropriate for you. I also explore an important option when executing these processes that may not have an intuitive behavior from the eyes of a PL/SQL developer.

The chapter concludes by introducing JavaScript Object Notation (JSON) as a way to return heterogeneous information back to the browser instead of returning a basic text string.

A Brief History of AJAX

The term *AJAX* was first publicly stated in 2005 by Jesse James Garrett in an article titled "Ajax: A New Approach to Web Applications." Garrett described it in relation to Google Suggest, a tool that started providing suggestions as you type. This is exactly what's going on in the employee search example shown in Chapter 5.

■ **Note** A copy of the Garrett article can be found at www.adaptivepath.com/ideas/ajax-new-approach-web-applications/

AJAX is short for *aynchronous JavaScript and XML,* and it's a combination of the two technologies. Despite its name, AJAX doesn't need to be asynchronous and the use of XML isn't required. JSON is often used as an alternative data transmission format. Both points are explored later in the chapter.

Google further pushed the technology with Gmail and Google Maps, but its precursor was Microsoft's ActiveX control in Internet Explorer 5. It's now used heavily in tools such as APEX, and a few options are available to the developer.

Figure 9-1 illustrates the classic synchronous web application model with an AJAX call representing a validation or extra fetch of data after the page has been loaded.

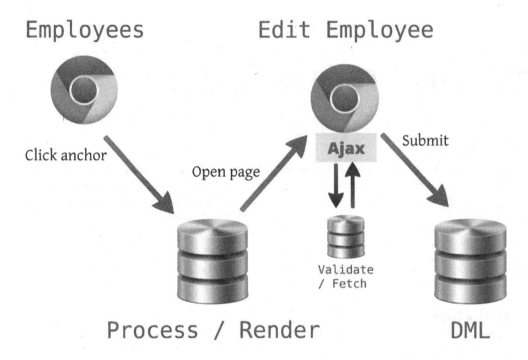

Figure 9-1. *Classic synchronous web application model*

Preparing the APEX Page

The four options described below can all be demonstrated by executing a dynamic action on click of a button that will fetch a value from the database based on a provided value. The page at runtime will look similar to Figure 9-2, where a user can type an employee number, click a button, and see the salary without page submission.

Process
Some emps: 7369, 7900, 7902

Empno	7900
Sal	950

Old	DA	Deferred	JSON

Figure 9-2. *Page UI to demonstrate options in this chapter*

■ **Note**   I included some HTML in the region definition as a reminder of some employee numbers and modified the grid layout of the buttons to tidy the page.

First, create a new blank page with one HTML region called *Process*.

Now create two items to the region. If you're using the EMP table, create an P9_EMPNO and P9_SAL field; alternatively, any ID/value pair will do.

Finally, create four buttons whose action will be *Defined by Dynamic Action*. The relevant dynamic actions will be detailed in the next section so just leave default attributes for now, but name them Old, DA, Deferred, and JSON respectively.

All buttons will trigger a relevant dynamic action (defined below) that will invoke in some form what's termed a *PL/SQL callback*. This means it's possible to execute some follow up JavaScript based on the success or failure of the PL/SQL, but some options provide flexibility where others do not.

Choosing Process Options

A number of options for invoking AJAX are present in the APEX environment. All are worth noting as you may encounter older code. It's good to be aware of the options available to make the best decision for your particular environment, though at times it's solely up to developer preference.

The Old htmldb_Get

The htmldb_Get function was available since APEX 3.x and, while undocumented, it was generally accepted as the method for invoking an APEX application process. Thanks to backward compatibility, you may find this method still used in APEX applications but it's recommended to refactor the code to use supported libraries.

Applying the Functionality

Create a dynamic action to execute JavaScript on click of the *Old* button, using Listing 9-1 as the source. Ensure the Fire on Page Load property is unchecked.

Listing 9-1. Deprecated AJAX Method

```
console.log('Old process');
var ajaxRequest = new htmldb_Get
  (null
  ,$v('pFlowId')
  ,'APPLICATION_PROCESS=CB_OLD'
  ,$v('pFlowStepId')
);
ajaxRequest.addParam('x01', $v('P9_EMPNO'));
var ajaxReturn = ajaxRequest.get();
console.log('Return:'+ajaxReturn);
$s('P9_SAL',ajaxReturn);
```

This JavaScript defines a new request that will invoke a PL/SQL application process called CB_OLD. The addParam() function adds the value from empno field into a pre-defined parameter x01 that will be available to retrieve in PL/SQL.

Finally the JavaScript then executes the process and sets the return value to the salary field.

Figure 9-3 shows where the PL/SQL callbacks are managed in the Page Designer.

Figure 9-3. *AJAX Callbacks are PL/SQL programs*

Right click here to create a new process called CB_OLD, ensuring the computation point is *AJAX Callback*. Use Listing 9-2 as the process source.

Listing 9-2. PL/SQL Callback for the Old Button

```
begin
  apex_debug.message('x01:'||apex_application.g_x01);
  select sal
  into :P9_SAL
  from emp
  where empno = to_number(apex_application.g_x01);
  htp.prn(:P9_SAL);
exception when no_data_found then
  htp.prn('?');
end;
```

In versions prior to APEX 4.x, this would be an application level process defined in Shared Components.

The PL/SQL process will be similar across these options, but the method of receiving information can vary. In this case the empno value added to parameter x01 is now accessible using the supplied package variable apex_application.g_x01. There are 10 such variables available for static input all defined as VARCHAR2(32767), so a an explicit conversion to number is appropriate.

The salary value is returned to the JavaScript call using the supplied API htp.prn(). Any data supplied to this function accumulates in the returned result as a text string. More examples of this as we go along.

If the supplied employee number is not found, then a PL/SQL exception is caught and, in this case, a question mark is returned instead.

Problems with This htmldb_Get

The method is fully functional and handles a number of variations to inputting and outputting data. However, it's deprecated and never officially supported, and there are new purpose built handlers available.

In general it is not good practice to use undocumented functions. Some do become available over time, but you should now find them appearing in the APEX namespaces such as apex.da.resume.

Declarative Dynamic Actions

APEX 4.x made AJAX communication with the database declarative by introducing dynamic action functionality. The same task can now be solved using more declarative attributes and a slightly modified PL/SQL block.

Applying the Functionality

A PL/SQL action replaces the JavaScript call to a PL/SQL callback, so select accordingly when creating an on click dynamic action for the DA button.

The declarative APEX functionality does all the hard work while you can define the incoming and outgoing parameters of the AJAX call within the action definition, as represented in Figure 9-4. Note none of the actions in this chapter need to Fire on Page Load.

Figure 9-4. *PL/SQL process called from dynamic action*

The PL/SQL code used is available in Listing 9-3. The page item can be referenced directly as bind variable, but the value is only communicated to the database from the browser if listed in Page Items to Submit.

Listing 9-3. PL/SQL Code for Dynamic Action

```
begin
  apex_debug.message('P9_EMPNO:'||:P9_EMPNO);
  select sal
  into :P9_SAL
  from emp
  where empno = to_number(:P9_EMPNO);
exception when no_data_found then
  :P9_SAL := '?';
end;
```

Therefore, the page items to submit/return represent the input/output parameters respectively. Page Items to Return will re-populate the browser with any variables updated within the PL/SQL block. Both can be comma delimited lists.

If PL/SQL is migrated to packages, which should happen for the majority of application code, page items should be sent as parameters to procedures.

```
my_proc(p_value => :P1_ITEM);
```

If necessary, session state can be accessed using the functions such as nv('P9_EMPNO'), but ideally procedures should be able to execute independent of an APEX session to help testing.

If P9_SAL had it's own on change event, then the Suppress Change Event property can stop it from being invoked. Further down the property list under Execution Options the Wait For Result attribute defines whether this particular action is synchronous or asynchronous, but more on this in a later section. When checked, the subsequent action won't execute until the PL/SQL has finished.

Finding Balance between Dynamic Actions and jQuery

While dynamic actions make AJAX functionality accessible to even those learning APEX, there are some shortfalls. They provide the ability to alternate between JavaScript and PL/SQL, but the path provided by action sequences is linear. Control information needs to be included within parameter passing to conditionally execute code rather than doing so declaratively, limiting flexibility.

In larger, more complex pages, care needs to be taken to modularize the code, yet even so the developer can waste time clicking through different action properties to read the flow of code. Compare this to containing all logic within a block of jQuery.

At the end of the day, however, dynamic actions provide rapid development capability while obfuscating complexity. You can use the best of both worlds with dynamic actions providing the framework with while most of your JavaScript and PL/SQL code lives elsewhere.

Using apex.server.process

To enable PL/SQL to be invoked from JavaScript, APEX provides a wrapper to jQuery.ajax() called apex.server.process. All the features available via dynamic action are available as attributes.

Applying the Functionality

Invoking a PL/SQL process from JavaScript is truly the bridge between the two technologies. Given the previous examples to compare with, the syntax is easy to adapt. The difficult part is getting used to the behaviours of JavaScript, especially compared to what you may be used to with PL/SQL.

JavaScript

The JavaScript utilized for the click action on the Deferred button is found in Listing 9-4. The following step will be to define the PL/SQL callback the method executes, the name CB_AJAX is set as the first parameter.

Listing 9-4. AJAX Call Using APEX-Supplied Wrapper

```
console.log('Before');
apex.server.process
  ("CB_AJAX" // name of AJAX callback
  ,{ // pData
      x01      : $v('P9_EMPNO')
     ,pageItems : '#P9_EMPNO'
   }
  ,{ // pOptions
      dataType:"text" // default: json
     ,loadingIndicator : "#P9_SAL"
   }
).done(function(pData) {
  // PL/SQL finished
  console.log('Success');

  $s('P9_SAL', pData);
});
console.log('End');
```

The second parameter shows two methods for sending information to the PL/SQL unit. Values can be explicitly assigned to the `application.g_x01` variables or `v('APP_AJAX_X01')` substitution string. Alternatively a comma-delimited list of page items can be supplied, identified using ID selectors. The browser values for these page items will be submitted to session state, referenced using `v('P9_EMPNO')`. Note the similarity between the JavaScript version of the function `$v('P9_EMPNO')`.

Information coming back from PL/SQL is handled differently when using this method. Information from PL/SQL is streamed into an output parameter. The third parameter can dictate the expected format of this output. The default is JSON, but here I've set it to `text` to allow a simple value be used to set P9_SAL., The JSON default will be demonstrated in a later section.

The `.done()` method is why the button in this example is Deferred. It only executes only upon return from the PL/SQL function, then sets the browser item P9_SAL using the APEX supplied `$s()` function. The fact it is the callback to the PL/SQL call can cause confusion in the JavaScript as the code will keep processing, not waiting for the PL/SQL to return. The output will actually be:

```
Before
End
Success
```

This reason alone will impact workflow design. It eliminates synchronisity from web application interactions, a style of coding prevalant in stateful environments like Oracle Forms. Loopholes that attain synchronous communication are being tightened as it's considered bad practice in a web environment. More on this behaviour later in the chapter.

Alternative JavaScript solutions

Given the flexibility jQuery offers, there are a number of ways the same task could be written. It's mostly down the developer preferences, but it's also recommended to listen to the documentation regarding deprecated functions.

Listing 9-5 demonstrates the same functionality but with the .done() function deferred until the end to highlight the nature of the code. The code is now more representative of the chronological behaviour, with a few more console logs for clarity.

Listing 9-5. Deferred jQuery function

```
console.log('Before');
var jqxhr = apex.server.process
  ("CB_AJAX" // name of AJAX callback
  ,{ // pData
     x01       : $v('P9_EMPNO')
     ,pageItems : '#P9_EMPNO'
   }
  ,{ // pOptions
     dataType:"text" // default: json
     ,loadingIndicator : "#P9_SAL"
   }
);
console.log(Process Submitted');

jqxhr.done(function(data) {
    // wait for result content here
    console.log('Success');

});
console.log('End');
```

The output would read as follows:

```
Before
Process Submitted
End
Success
```

Note the JavaScript executes to the end, but only invokes the .done() function once the process is complete. Two other functions are relevant here, .fail() and .always(). The .done() function will only fire on successful completion, where .always() will execute regardless of the outcome. The .fail() function will execute when the data doesn't match the defined data type. If the JSON is invalid this can help with debugging. Be aware that PL/SQL exceptions will not invoke .fail(), they will just modify the output data content.

If the function names sound familiar, it's because there are deprecated synonyms that will still honour executions that look more like the following:

```
apex.server.process
  ("CB_DEPRECATED"
  ,{ // pData
    pageItems : '#P1_ITEM'
   }
```

```
  ,{ // pOptions
    success:function(pData){
      // wait for result content here
      console.log('Success');
    }
   }
);
```

As apex.server.process is a wrapper to .ajax() and a shorthand version in .post(). You may encounter calls that look similar but do the same thing:

```
var ajaxData =
 {"p_request"      : "APPLICATION_PROCESS=CB_AJAX"
 ,"p_flow_id"      : $v('pFlowId')
 ,"p_flow_step_id" : $v('pFlowStepId')
 ,"p_instance"     : $v('pInstance')
 ,"x01"            : $v('P9_EMPNO')
};

$.ajax({"url" : 'wwv_flow.show'
  ,"data" : ajaxData
  ,"settings" : {"type":"POST","dataType":"text"}
       })
  .done(function(pData){
    console.log('pData:'+pData);
    $s('P9_SAL', pData);
  }
);
```

I recommend the documented methods

Creating the PL/SQL callback

Create an AJAX callback called CB_AJAX using Listing 9-6 as the PL/SQL. This is the process invoked from apex.server.process.

Data can be read from either the apex_application variables or from the page item bind variables, depending on how the information was set in the jQuery call.

Listing 9-6. PL/SQL Callback for the AJAX Method

```
begin
  apex_debug.message('x01:'||apex_application.g_x01);
  apex_debug.message('P9_EMPNO:'||:P9_EMPNO);
  select sal
  into :P9_SAL
  from emp
  where empno = to_number(:P9_EMPNO);
  htp.prn(:P9_SAL);
exception when no_data_found then
  htp.prn('?');
end;
```

Information is returned by sending data using htp.prn(), which is sent to the success function as the parameter referred to as pData.

Considerations regarding Use of apex.server.process

A clear advantage of this method is the flexibility it provides, giving the developer complete control over how and when code executes.

Another benefit is the program logic is available in the one location. The direct antithesis is the extra skill set required to interpret and understand the surrounding JavaScript.

The trick is to find the right balance for your team and your application between dynamic actions and explicit jQuery.

Consider the illusion of snappiness

On my slow Australian internet connection means it can take a few moments to process AJAX calls. If you don't have a slow connection you can simulate one using the browser device mode. Mobile device users won't have the high speed WiFi developers in the office enjoy, so it's good to review your application with speed throttled, as shown in Figure 9-5.

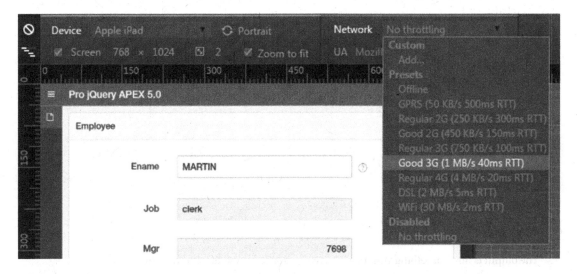

Figure 9-5. *Throttle connection in browser device mode*

Doing so should help you consider the importance of every AJAX call and how it affects your workflow. Combining or reducing network traffic is best, an issue with which Oracle Forms programmers would be familiar.

Async vs. Sync

A frequent "gotcha" while learning JavaScript relates to the timing of callback behavior. APEX handles some of this complexity with the Wait For Result option in a PL/SQL dynamic action.

If you modify the DA example to use this feature as of APEX 5.0.2 you will see a message in the console as shown in Figure 9-6.

Figure 9-6. *Browser feature deprecation warning*

This message is not unique to Oracle APEX. The declarative feature currently utilises the `async` jQuery parameter and browsers are giving fair warning to developers to meet W3C specifications, in this case the APEX development team.

The solution will be to refactor the dynamic action framework to use the deferred actions. In future this may be done using native HTML "promises", once browser support is ubiquitous.

Modifying the example in Listing 9-4 by setting the `async` parameter to false is equivalent to checking the Wait For Result option in the dynamic action:

```
console.log('Before');
apex.server.process
  ("CB_AJAX" // name of AJAX callback
  ,{ // pData
     x01       : $v('P9_EMPNO')
     ,pageItems : '#P9_EMPNO'
  }
  ,{ // pOptions
     dataType:"text" // default: json
     ,async: true
     ,loadingIndicator : "#P9_SAL"
  }
).done(function(pData) {
  // PL/SQL finished
  console.log('Success');

  $s('P9_SAL', pData);
});
console.log('End');
```

The output is now something you may intuitively expect complete with warning.

```
Before
Synchronous XMLHttpRequest on the main thread is deprecated because of its detrimental
effects to the end user's experience. For more help, check http://xhr.spec.whatwg.org/.
Success
End
```

For this reason, code flow becomes more vividly apparent when written as jQuery instead of a set of dynamic actions.

Synchronous behavior modifies the output of the JavaScript by making execution more linear/chronological, but this behaviour has limited uses in web applications. The deferred functions should be logically considered as just a forked execution block and doesn't need to be synchronous.

Oracle will modify its underlying code for the dynamic action Wait for Result property accordingly over time. For a more detailed discussion on how this parameter affects the APEX environment, visit John Snyders' post:

http://hardlikesoftware.com/weblog/2015/04/15/apex-and-asynchronous-ajax/

To summarize, if you rely on synchronous behavior for your AJAX calls, you're designing your application wrong.

JSON Output

Discrete units of output data are useful when defining workflow for user interface events. However, larger data sets are commonly fed to visual web component such as charts.

JSON is an object notation that's so ubiquitous it's become further embedded in the API frameworks supplied with APEX 5.

Prior to APEX 5, there were some undocumented functions that made it easy to send data from PL/SQL back to JavaScript as a JSON data object.

Applying the Functionality

The infrastructure is similar to the previous option. Listing 9-7 shows how a SQL query can be written out as a JSON object using the apex_json supplied PL/SQL package. This becomes the AJAX callback CB_JSON.

Listing 9-7. PL/SQL Callback "CB_JSON"

```
declare
    c sys_refcursor;
begin
  apex_debug.message(':P9_EMPNO => '||:P9_EMPNO);

  open c for select empno, ename, job, hiredate, sal from emp where empno = :P9_EMPNO;
  apex_json.write(c);
end;
```

The JavaScript in Listing 9-8 demonstrates how this data can be processed as an array of records. It is the JavaScript action for the dynamic action on the JSON button.

Listing 9-8. Ajax Call Receiving JSON Data

```
console.log('before');
apex.server.process
  ("CB_JSON"
  ,{ // pData
    pageItems : '#P9_EMPNO'
   }
).done(function(pData){
    console.log('Success');
    console.log(pData);
    console.log(pData[0]);
    console.log(pData[0].ENAME);
```

```
        console.log(pData[0].JOB);
        console.log(pData[0].HIREDATE);

        $s('P9_SAL', pData[0].SAL);
});
console.log('End');
```

Note the attributes of the record in the array are named after the columns in the query. JSON objects can be constructed manually and may need to be referenced differently. Outputting the data object via console.log will allow you to determine the layout of a given JSON object, as shown in Figure 9-7.

Figure 9-7. *Console log displaying JSON object*

Further JSON examples can be found in Chapter 13, receiving information from the database and showing how a function can quickly populate fields on page.

Summary

A number of options are available to the APEX developer to invoke PL/SQL from an event on the web page. This allows the user to interact with the page in a powerful way.

Communication between browser and database server is a web problem and certain constraints can ultimately direct the workflow of an application. Remember, APEX is an optimistic environment. Workflow typically consists of an attempt to do something with the expectation of success, then respond to failure.

The major challenge lies in utilizing declarative dynamic actions or coding the logic within jQuery. Learning the balance between skill set, readability, and maintenance does not happen overnight, but does give the developer a choice of different scenarios.

Many factors may impact the decision from quantity of input and outputs, to layout of the page, to business logic required upon return of the data. The JSON notation allows larger sets of data to be sent to other frameworks such as those building charts.

■ ■ ■

Link a Check Box to a Collection

This chapter presents the first practical application of the techniques explored so far. Consider adding items to an online shopping cart. The list of items can have a check box, each allowing the user to add to the data store.

The resulting APEX page will combine several fundamental components serving the AJAX mechanism, allowing the report to insert a record into the database the moment the user clicks on the page.

This chapter also offers insight in the use of APEX debugging to track any runtime errors you may encounter.

About APEX Collections

APEX collections provide the perfect mechanism for the cart. They are session-based tables ideal for transient data with a variety of data APIs. Since global temporary tables do not work with the APEX session pooling architecture, APEX collections are the ideal replacement. They are simply a pair of regular database tables that include the APEX session ID.

This information is exposed to the developer with the dictionary view apex_collections. The view combines a data-set name with a set of generically named columns with a variety of data types, 50 character columns plus 5 dates, 5 numbers, and a CLOB.

PL/SQL APIs are used to populate the view. A variety of methods are available, depending on the quantity and structure of the data being updated.

This example will use a check box as the mechanism to add or subtract from the APEX collection, which is the shopping cart. This method shows how tightly coupled all the components can be, and I identify an area that could be extended.

Extending the Report

Several methods are available for adding a check box to the Employees report page. The method described in this chapter uses simple concepts and makes good use of the features of the database and the APEX product.

Add Column to SQL

Edit the report region source to include a new column in the SQL. This column uses a scalar subquery to read from the APEX dictionary view apex_collections. If the employee number from the table matches data saved in the collection, then the checked attribute will be included in the render of the check box, as shown in Listing 10-1.

Listing 10-1. Check Box Added to Report SQL

```
select "EMPNO",
"ENAME",
"JOB",
"MGR",
"HIREDATE",
"SAL",
"COMM",
"DEPTNO",
 -- set attribute if empno present in collection
 -- (see column html expression)
 (select 'checked="checked"'
  from apex_collections
  where collection_name = 'CHECKOUT'
  and    n001 = empno) AS ajax_checkbox
from "#OWNER#"."EMP"
```

The collection name CHECKOUT represents the name used to identify the data set used for the cart.

Edit the Report Column

Edit the properties of the ajax_checkbox column and start by renaming the column heading to Add to Cart.

Set the HTML Expression of the column to form a check box input item, each with a value of the relevant employee number substituted in with hash tags surrounding the column alias #EMPNO#:

```
<input type="checkbox" #AJAX_CHECKBOX# value="#EMPNO#" name="f42" id="f42_#ROWNUM#"/>
```

The check box is checked if the scalar subquery finds a record in the collection as the data returned is embedded within the HTML expression as #AJAX_CHECKBOX#, referring to the relevant column alias.

To stay consistent with the format of APEX tabular forms, the name attribute is a number up to 200 prefixed with "f." The Id is suffix with the row number to stay unique for the page. I choose 42 because it's usually out of the range of any declarative form columns that may already exist, and it has enough cultural significance to allow code readers to join the dots, particularly in a small page like this one.

Listening for the Click Event

Add a dynamic action Toggle Check Box that listens for change on the following jQuery selector that identifies the relevant classic report and only the check boxes within it:

```
#p2_emps :checkbox[name="f42"]
```

This simplified selector would also work, but it would not be selective enough if other check boxes are added to the report:

```
#p2_emps :checkbox
```

The JavaScript action will invoke the PL/SQL process to manipulate the collection, ensure it's not called on page load.

Listing 10-2 describes a PL/SQL callback being invoked, sending the value of $(this.triggeringElement). It's an attribute supplied by the dynamic action that represents the check box that triggered the change event.

Listing 10-2. JavaScript Invoking AJAX Call to PL/SQL

```
// send the value of the checkbox (pk) and if it's checked
apex.server.process
  ("CB_CHECKOUT"
  ,{ // pData
    x01 : $(this.triggeringElement).val()
    ,x02 : $(this.triggeringElement).prop('checked')
  }
  ,{ // pOptions
    dataType:"text"
    ,success:function(pData){
      console.log('Return:'+pData);
    }
  }
);
```

The PL/SQL function can return information into pData using the htp API. This information could form or dictate a response to the user.

Adding PL/SQL Processes

The listener on the check box will invoke a PL/SQL process that needs to toggle whether that item is included in the collection. Doing so provides an opportunity to utilize the APEX debugging tools.

Create PL/SQL Callback

Create an AJAX callback named CB_CHECKOUT using the code in Listing 10-3. The parameters can be referenced using global variables in the apex_application supplied package.

If the check box is checked and the property is true, an entry is added to the collection named CHECKOUT. The first character and first number field in the collection are set to the value of the check box and the empno respectively.

If the check box is not checked, an API is called to remove an entry with the first attribute equal to the value supplied.

Listing 10-3. PL/SQL Process to Toggle Collection Membership

```
/* toggle collection membership */ apex_debug.message('CB_CHECKOUT');
apex_debug.message('CB_CHECKOUT');
apex_debug.message('CB_CHECKOUT');
apex_debug.message('Value:'||apex_application.g_x01);
apex_debug.message('Checked:'||apex_application.g_x02);

-- add member to collection if checked
-- else delete where c001 = value
if apex_application.g_x02 = 'true' then
  APEX_COLLECTION.ADD_MEMBER
```

```
   (p_collection_name => 'CHECKOUT'
   ,p_c001 => apex_application.g_x01
   ,p_n001 => apex_application.g_x01
   );
   htp.prn('added:'||apex_application.g_x01);
else
  APEX_COLLECTION.DELETE_MEMBERS
   (p_collection_name => 'CHECKOUT'
   ,p_attr_number => 1
   ,p_attr_value => apex_application.g_x01
   );
   htp.prn('removed:'||apex_application.g_x01);
end if;
```

At this point, these API calls will return an error since the collection has not yet been created, though it does provide an opportunity to follow the debug trail.

Debug Mode

Run the page in debug mode and open the JavaScript console. Then click on a check box. The console in Figure 10-1 indicates the dynamic action Toggle Check Box was executed. The following line shows an error propogated from PL/SQL indicating the collection does not exist:

```
Return:sqlerrm:ORA-20102: Application collection CHECKOUT does not exist
```

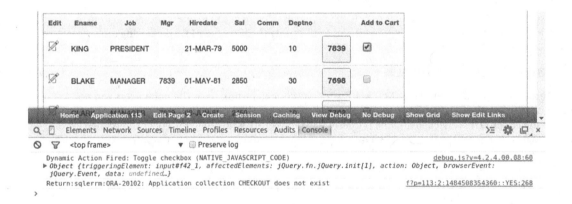

Figure 10-1. *Console window after clicking a check box*

Click the View Debug link on the developer toolbar and open the debug entry that mentions CB_CHECKOUT in the path info column. Scroll to the end and find the PL/SQL errors, as shown in Figure 10-2.

0.53100	0.03100	Run APPLICATION_PROCESS= request	4	
0.56200	0.12500	...Execute Statement: begin /* toggle collection membership */ apex_debug.message('CB_CHECKOUT'); apex_debug.message('Value:'||apex_application.g_x01); apex_debug.message('Checked:'||apex_application.g_x02); -- add member to collection if checked -- else delete where c001 = value if apex_application.g_x02 = 'true' then APEX_COLLECTION.ADD_MEMBER (p_collection_name => 'CHECKOUT' ,p_c001 => apex_application.g_x01 ,p_n001 => apex_application.g_x01); htp.prn(' added'); else APEX_COLLECTION.DELETE_MEMBERS (p_collection_name => 'CHECKOUT' ,p_attr_number => 1 ,p_attr_value => apex_application.g_x01); htp.prn('removed'); end if; end;	4	
0.68700	0.00000	CB_CHECKOUT	4	
0.68700	0.00000	Value:7839	4	
0.68700	0.07800	Checked:true	4	
0.76500	0.00000	Collection - Getting collection ID for Collection Name: CHECKOUT	4	
0.76500	0.01500	Collection - Returning Collection ID for Collection Name: CHECKOUT	4	
0.78000	0.00000	Logging exception: Sqlerrm: ORA-20102: Application collection CHECKOUT does not exist Backtrace: ORA-06512: at "APEX_040200.WWV_FLOW_COLLECTION", line 3011	2	
0.78000	0.01600	Logging exception: Sqlerrm: ORA-20102: Application collection CHECKOUT does not exist Backtrace: ORA-06512: at "SYS.WWV_DBMS_SQL", line 1091 ORA-06512: at "APEX_040200.WWV_FLOW_DYNAMIC_EXEC", line 832 ORA-06512: at "APEX_040200.WWV_FLOW_PPR_UTIL", line 173	2	
0.79600	0.00000	Stop APEX Engine detected	4	
0.79600	-	Final commit	4	-

Figure 10-2. Debug log indicating where the error occurred

In larger applications, this provides an easy way to track where an error occurred and, perhaps, determine why. Note the calls to apex_debug.message have noted what callback was invoked and what the parameter values where.

Initialise Collection

To resolve the error, the collection must be created when the page loads, before the user starts interacting.

Create a Pre-Rendering PL/SQL process with processing point Before Header, using PL/SQL in Listing 10-4. This creates the collection if it doesn't already exist. The PL/SQL callback may now safely manipulate the collection.

Listing 10-4. PL/SQL Initialization on Page Load

```
/* create empty collection if not already present */
if not apex_collection.collection_exists('CHECKOUT') then
  apex_collection.create_collection
  (p_collection_name => 'CHECKOUT');
end if;
```

■ **Caution**   Be careful when selecting the API to do this task. A viable alternative would be apex_collection. create_or_truncate_collection, but that would mean clearing the cart if the user refreshed the page.

Note in Figure 10-3 the APEX documentation describes the APIs clearly and concisely. It's worth familiarizing yourself with these pages as they provide a good resource.

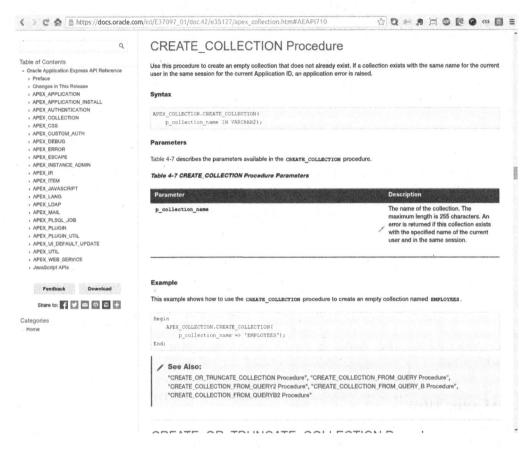

Figure 10-3. *Useful and concise APEX documentation*

Session Information

Click on the Session link in the developer bar and set the view on Collections. As shown in Figure 10-4, both records checked are present in the collection, which is actually a table in the database.

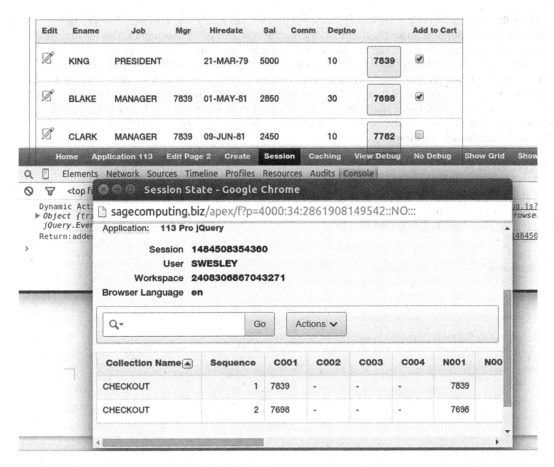

Figure 10-4. *Collection data shown in Session State pop-up window*

Uncheck one of the boxes and then refresh the collection list and see the instant feedback.

User Feedback

The success function from Listing 10-2 displays the information sent to `htp.prn()`, which is now available via the success function's input paramter `pData`.

```
success:function(pData){
    console.log('Return:'+pData);
}
```

This information isn't much use to the user in the JavaScript console, nor is it practical to reference in any subsequent action in the dynamic actions since they are not conditional.

A common solution is to provide some form of messaging system to the user. There are a number of jQuery frameworks, or you could import a notification APEX plug-in to display an alert if a hidden item is changed on the page.

The following solution might not satisfy JavaScript purests, but it shows a method to convert the callback output to a notification for the user that demonstrates related APEX mechanics. This example uses tha native alert, but further exploration into client messaging continues in the next chapter.

Create Global Page (formerly known as Page Zero) in your application,and then add a Static Content region using the Blank with Attributes template. Add a hidden item P0_SIGNAL and set Value Protected to No.

Create a dynamic action on change of P0_SIGNAL with a condition checking for not null. Create a new dynamic action on the global page called Receive Signal, which runs JavaScript on change of P0_SIGNAL. The JavaScript sends the signal value to the native alert, thereby allowing feedback of information from the database process back to the browser:

```
alert($v('P0_SIGNAL'));
```

A subsequent action can clear the P0_SIGNAL item, but ensure Suppress Change Event is set to Yes. Otherwise, the page will invoke an infinite loop as the dynamic action changes the value of the same item to which it listens for change. (See Figure 10-5.)

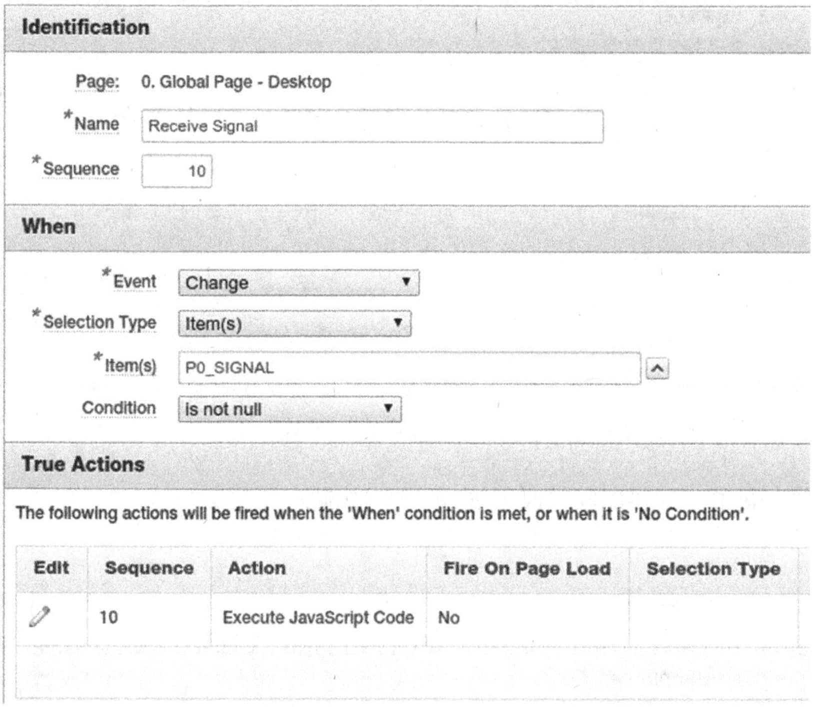

Figure 10-5. *Dynamic action listening for signal*

Finally, return to the Employees page and append the following after the console.log in the success function in the call to apex.server.process:

```
$s('P0_SIGNAL', pData);
```

Now clicking on a check box in the report invokes a set of activity:

- Dynamic action responds to check box change

- JavaScript action invokes AJAX callback

- PL/SQL function adds or removes entry from APEX collection

- Successful return from function call sets PO_SIGNAL

- Global page dynamic action converts signal to user feedback

You should also see success message in the browser console.

Summary

Now that you are aware of all the components necessary to allow the database to communicate, it's a matter of working out the best ways to apply these behaviors.

In this chapter, you added a check box column source from an APEX collection. You then added all the components required to add or remove an element to the collection when the check box was toggled.

It doesn't take much of a stretch of the imagination to transform any of these components into something similar to manage other user interface scenarios.

CHAPTER 11

■ ■ ■

Using jQuery Dialogs

Since APEX delivers web pages, it naturally provides a simple interface to the browser dialogs and alerts; however, they are bareboned. jQuery offers a more polished set of dialogs that facilitate alerts and questions that can match the application's theme.

This chapter shows how to replace the default Delete dialog in the Employees form with a jQuery style dialog. The chapter concludes by demonstrating how the dialog text could be sourced from the database.

The Undo Alternative

A user interface design alternative for dialogs is to provide an undo feature. Trust the users in their actions, but provide a temporary ability to undo. Figure 11-1 shows Gmail's option to undo deletes.

The conversation has been moved to the Trash. Undo

Figure 11-1. *Gmail temporarily offers users the ability to undo their deletes*

E-mail folder structure also offers deleted e-mails in the bin once the temporary message is left behind. For some applications, undo behavior can be difficult or is out of context. Systems such as those involving payments will have steps that cannot be undone.

A fuller discourse on the matter is beyond the scope of this book, but one can be found at http://alistapart.com/article/neveruseawarning. I would add the recommendation that dialogs use verbs on their buttons. In other words, use "doing words" such as *Send* or *Discard*, but not *Okay*.

The interface may not even call for a stop/continue request, but rather a decision between options. Perhaps a formal acknowledgment might be required, or the user could be forced to change selection from the default dialog button before continuing.

The Browser Solution

All browsers offer a simple, effective modal dialog box invoked with the confirm() command. Oracle APEX provides a wrapper to this function, offering a second parameter to define request value used in page processing.

```
apex.confirm('Delete this record?', 'DELETE');
```

This is the same call used with the Delete button. It can be extended further to include other documented options.

```
apex.confirm("Save Setting?", {
  request:"SAVE"
 ,set:{"P1_DEPTNO":10, "P1_EMPNO":1234}
 ,showWait:true
});
```

Dynamic actions include confirm and alert actions that will invoke the same APIs.

The rendering of the native dialog will vary depending on the browser. Because some wouldn't be considered user friendly, they are in need of customization. Figure 11-2 shows the dialog shown when invoking the Delete button on the Employee form. The only element that's customizable is the message text. Also note that Chrome has flipped the position of the Cancel and OK buttons, shifting the default to OK.

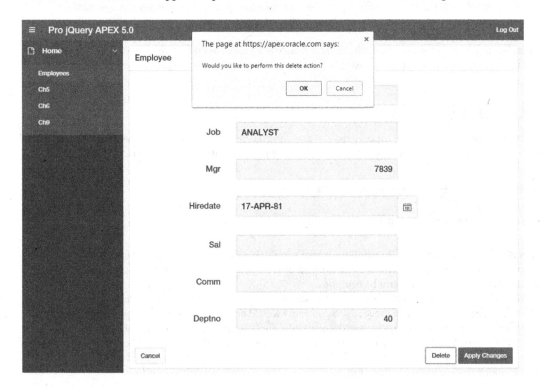

Figure 11-2. *Browser window.confim() method*

Another consideration is, in my case, Chrome interrupted all tabs open within the browser, waiting for a response. Some other browsers operate independently within the tab.

jQuery Dialogs

jQuery dialogs are coupled with the jQueryUI theme so they will match the interface and have a more polished finish. They are heavily customizable and do not disrupt other browser tabs.

This section demonstrates a solution that could be customized to suit all the scenarios mentioned earlier. At the conclusion of the chapter, we will provide a simpler, more generic solution.

Priming the Dialog

This method adds a DIV to the page body that will be transformed into a dialog box, ready to be invoked on demand. Add Listing 11-1 as *Executed when Page Loads* for the Employee form.

Listing 11-1. On Load JavaScript for APEX Form Page

```
/* add catalyst div to page body */
$('body').append('<div id="confirm_delete" />')
/* turn div into dialog */
$("#confirm_delete").dialog(
    {modal : true
    ,title : 'Confirm delete'
    ,autoOpen:false
    ,resizable:false
    ,dialogClass: "no-close"
    ,width : '300px'
    ,closeOnEscape : false
    ,buttons : {
      "Cancel" : function () {
        $(this).dialog("close");
      }
      ,"Delete": function () {
        $(this).dialog("close");
        apex.submit('DELETE');
      }
    }
});
```

The dialog function has some relatively self-explanatory attributes, plus explicit instructions for each button defined. Both close the dialog, and the latter also submits the page as DELETE.

No dialog is invoked at this point—it's just preparing the DOM for use.

Opening the Dialog

The call to invoke the dialog is not a function, but a method on the DIV. The HTML within the DIV forms the dialog message, so it may be set at any time using .html(). The button's actions are defined as callbacks within the dialog definition.

Listing 11-2 is a function that accepts a message parameter, sets the HTML, and then opens the dialog. These actions are chained in the one statement for performance. This function is to be defined in the Function and Variable Declaration section, but will be invoked from the Delete button.

Listing 11-2. Function Declaration for Form Page

```
/* open delete dialog */
function delete_dialog(p_msg) {
  $('#confirm_delete')
    .css('margin','12px') // tidy the messsage within the dialog
    .html(p_msg)          // define the actual message
    .dialog('open');      // open the dialog
}
```

Also included is some styling for the DIV to add some whitespace around the message text.

Alternatively, a call could be made to a PL/SQL process to determine the message, much like a PL/SQL validation *Function Returning Error Text*. This is demonstrated later in the chapter.

Calling the Function

The Delete button can now be modified to call the function, so modify the button's Target URL as the following:

```
javascript:delete_dialog("About to delete '"+$v('P3_ENAME')+"' <br><br>Are you sure?");
```

The function is invoked, passing the desired message string. This message includes the current value of the P3_ENAME field.

■ **Note** This sample code combines single and double quotes within strings. JavaScript accepts either punctuation set and, when used together, they offer different context within the string. This code surrounds the data in the employee name field with single quotes. The remainder of the literal text is surrounded with double quotes. This could be the other way around, or you can use the escape character "\" for literal quotes.

Figure 11-3 shows what the dialog looks like with the relevant DOM components in the developer toolbar.

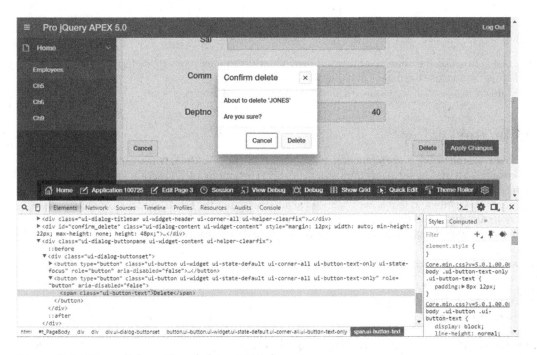

Figure 11-3. *jQuery dialog with underlying DOM elements*

Focus the Button

The JavaScript that invokes the dialog can be extended to ensure a certain button is focused by default, ready for the user. Currently the default is the Cancel button, which is ideal because it forces the user to make a decision.

It's possible to dictate this focus. The following code could be added after the dialog is opened to focus on the last button shown, ensuring the CSS class I spotted while tabbing through the buttons reflects the focus.

Reviewing Figure 11-3, you can see the class assigned to the button div container. Combining this with a pseudo-selector that returns the last child in a set of siblings, the button on the far right is selected.

```
$('div.ui-dialog-buttonset button:last').focus().css('ui-state-focus')
```

Customizing with CSS

Other visual customizations are possible with jQuery dialog boxes. In this case, I've drafted adjustments that will assist a user on a touch device.

Add Listing 11-3 to the page's *Inline CSS* attribute and adjustments are made as described in associated comments.

Listing 11-3. CSS to Modify Aspects of the Dialog Box

```
/* change right hand button colour */
div.ui-dialog-buttonset button:last-child  {
  background-color: #2578cf;
  color: white;
}

/* enlarge message font */
.ui-dialog-content {
  font-size:150%;
}
/* make buttons bolder and bigger (for fingers) */
div.ui-dialog-buttonset button {
  padding: 10px 14px;
}
div.ui-dialog-buttonset button span {
  font-weight:bold;
  font-size:150%;
}

/* give message text some elbow room */
div.ui-dialog {
  width: initial;
```

■ **Tip** These selectors were all found by navigating the elements of the dialog box using the browser tools, and then modifying or adding attributes on the fly to find the right selector.

Figure 11-4 shows the dialog box with the CSS customizations. The larger buttons are perfect for a touch-screen environment and the message is easier to read on a tablet.

Figure 11-4. *Customized jQuery dialog*

The Close button on the top right could also be hidden with CSS, but care needs to be taken not to affect other dialogs with such generic CSS.

Sourcing a Message from the Database

Before invoking the dialog, it is possible to source the displayed message from the database. Your business logic may even dictate certain circumstances where the dialog box is not relevant and an alert is shown instead when a particular record cannot be deleted.

The PL/SQL callback in Listing 11-4 demonstrates a hardcoded (naughty) check on the given employee number to see if it can be deleted. Based on this check. The callback returns two values in the JSON notation: an outcome and associated message. Use this code for an AJAX callback named CB_DELETE.

Listing 11-4. PL/SQL Callback for Delete Button

```
DECLARE
  l_outcome  VARCHAR2(20);
  l_message  VARCHAR2(200);
BEGIN
  apex_debug.message(':P3_EMPNO => '||:P3_EMPNO);

  IF :P3_EMPNO = 7839 THEN
    l_outcome := 'DENIED';
    l_message := 'Cannot delete the president';

  ELSE
    l_outcome := 'DELETE';

    SELECT 'Do you wish to delete '||ename||'?'
    INTO   l_message
    FROM   emp
    WHERE  empno = :P3_EMPNO;

  END IF;
```

```
   htp.p(
'{"output":[
    {"outcome":"'||l_outcome||'"
    ,"message":"'||l_message||'"
    }
]}'
);
END cb_delete;
```

The JavaScript in Listing 11-5 shows the delete employee function extended from a simple dialog request to invoke AJAX in order to determine what should happen next. The value in P3_EMPNO is submitted to session state and the JSON object is returned into pData.

The JSON object can be interrogated similar to an array that starts at index 0. In this case, there was only one entry and the attribute *outcome* is tested to determine whether to display the dialog or an alert.

Listing 11-5. Function to Open the Dialog and Focus the Cursor

```
/* employee delete button click */
function delete_dialog() {
 apex.server.process
   ("CB_DELETE"
   ,{ // pData
     //pageItems : '#P3_EMPNO'
    }
   ,{ // pOptions
     loadingIndicatorPosition: "page" // we're waiting for message, ensure user knows
    }
   ).done(
     function(pData){
       if (pData.output[0].outcome === 'DELETE') {
         // Set dialog based on output then display
         $('#confirm_delete')
           .css('margin','12px')
           .html(pData.output[0].message)
           .dialog('open');
         $('div.ui-dialog-buttonset button:last-child').focus();
       }
       else if (pData.output[0].outcome === 'DENIED') {
         // Notify user delete not allowed in this case
         alert(pData.output[0].message);
       }
   }); // end done
} // end delete_dialog
```

If the outcome was to DELETE, then the dialog is still called, but the message is first set from the returning value using the .htm() call. When DENIED, a browser alert is invoked instead with the returned message.

Defining a Generic Alert

The solution for the Delete button demonstrates rather specific customizations. Listing 11-6 shows a stand-alone function that displays a dialog, and executes a supplied callback function on click of the button.

Listing 11-6. Function to Display Generic Alert

```
/* display generic alert */
function get_alert (p_message, p_title, p_callback) {
  $("<div/>", { "html" : p_message})
     .attr({"title" : p_title})
     .css('margin','12px')
     .dialog({
        modal    : true
       ,buttons : {
          "Oh dear" : function() {
             $(this).dialog("close");
             // invoke function sent by invoker
             p_callback();
          }
       } // buttons
     }); // dialog
} // get_alert

function do_something(){
  // callback used for dialog button
  console.log('called');
}
```

The dialog can be invoked at any time using the following syntax:

```
get_alert('Hello Universe','Attention', do_something);
```

This example further demonstrates the variety of ways that tasks can be accomplished in jQuery.

Summary

Your user feedback framework could revolve around two or three parameterized library calls instead of native browser alerts. This allows for more flexible messages that fit with the style of your application.

Once again AJAX takes this concept even further by being able to interact with the database to help determine where events on the page lead.

That being said, this is but one workflow to be considered when designing your application. The alternative is to allow the users to undo their actions instead, pre-emptively warning them for a business rule that will still need to be rechecked upon user confirmation anyway.

■ ■ ■

Using Modal Forms

Modal forms are often useful in an enterprise setting to allow users to manage their data without traveling too far from where they found the record. Consider a pop up in a report that allows basic maintenance of record data.

The advent of APEX 5.0 revolutionizes the way complex modal forms are handled in APEX environments. Of course, not everyone will adopt APEX 5.0 straight away (I know some clients who still use APEX 3.x), and it's not the panacea of modal forms.

This chapter covers the middle ground of modal forms where the APEX developer has control over a simple set of items in a modal dialog to help manage application workflow.

A Brief History of Modal Forms in APEX

The usage of modal forms in APEX has changed as the product has matured. This doesn't mean one size fits all. There are still valid reasons to use each type of modal.

jQuery Modal

In the past, when using APEX 3.x the only way to show some form of dialog was to include the jQuery UI libraries and invoke a jQuery dialog. The same feature can be used today, without the need to worry about incorporating the libraries.

Figure 12-1 shows the example the website jQueryUI.com/dialog curated for modal forms. The sample code on the site is thorough, even providing validation for the fields generated within the JavaScript call.

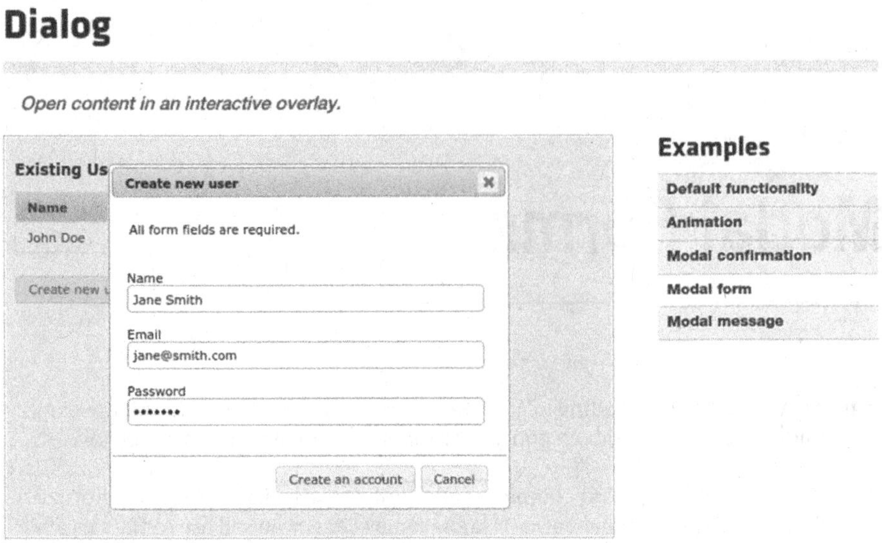

Dialog

Open content in an interactive overlay.

Figure 12-1. jQuery UI sample modal form

A problem with this solution is that it is JavaScript heavy. I have been encouraging you to find the right balance with the use of jQuery in APEX, and I don't recommend this as the first option to consider.

APEX Region Modal

Despite the wonderful improvements introduced with APEX 5 modal page types, APEX region modals are still a lightweight solution that integrates well with the database product. They are simply APEX regions with a specific template, hidden until invoked with a basic JavaScript call. APEX 5 made these regions easier to incorporate, and template options in the Universal Theme make them simple to adjust.

A number of the Oracle APEX Packaged Applications provide examples of region modals in use and are a great way to find suggested solutions for deconstruction. There is also a dedicated application demonstrating modal page types and template reigon modals.

Figure 12-2 shows an example from the Bug Tracker application. It shows how the region modal looks just like a standard form region, just within a modal dialog.

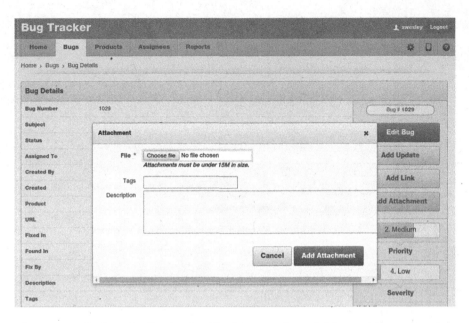

Figure 12-2. *Package Application Bug Tracker example modal form*

Instead of constructing your modal form with JavaScript, you define a region on the page and assign a specific region template allowing the region to behave like a modal. Then you can allocate items to the region, add buttons, and manage components just like a normal region.

Dynamic actions become involved to populate the region when invoked and process any data when closing. (I'll go into further detail later in the chapter.) Validation on closure is a disadvantage with this solution since it's not possible to use the page's declarative page-processing features.

SkillBuilder's Modal Page Plug-in

APEX plug-ins were introduced in APEX 4.0 as a way of extending the APEX product in a modularized but integrated manner. A number of software companies provide well-constructed APEX plug-ins with GPL/MIT licensing, which means you can utilize them within your projects free of charge. These plug-ins not only promote their author's brand but provide APEX developers with a greater set of resources. The team at SkillBuilders offer a plug-in that allows the developer to invoke a modal form that embeds a separate APEX page within the modal. At the time of writing, it is their most downloaded plug-in, though I suspect this will fade as APEX 5 becomes more prevalent. Figure 12-3 shows how an Interactive Report could be defined in the modal, since the modal is defined as a separate page.

Figure 12-3. *SkillBuilder online demo*

While this solution has a number of moving parts and can take a while to master, it offers greater flexibility in your applications and allows more complex modals to be constructed.

APEX 5

The ability to declaratively define modal dialogs has always been in the statement of direction for APEX 5, thanks to popular demand. The APEX 5 solution is essentially a fully integrated version of the SkillBuilders plug-in, where the APEX dev team have more flexibility.

Figure 12-4 shows a modal invoked within the APEX 5 sample application. When opened, you may notice a slight lag as the underlying modal page is generated from the database. The first two solutions would minimize any such lag as most of the rendering is done on the underlying page load.

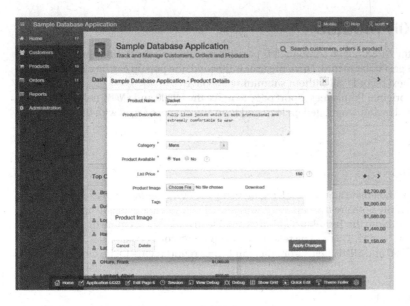

Figure 12-4. *APEX 5 declarative modal dialog*

The solution is completely declarative and has many features that are beyond the scope of this book. There will still be times where this solution may be considered overkill or APEX 5 may still be on the horizon for your site.

Selecting the Right Modal

Each of the solutions mentioned have advantages and disadvantages that have been summarized in Table 12-1.

Table 12-1. *Comparison of Modal Form Options*

	jQuery	APEX Region	Modal Plug-in	APEX 5.0
Major Skillset	JavaScript	APEX	Dynamic actions	**APEX**
Declarative	No	Mostly	To use	Yes
Prerendered (fast)	Yes	Yes	No	No
APEX version	3+	4+	4.x	5+
Complexity	High	Medium	Medium	Low
Flexibility	Low	Medium	High	High
Utilize Page Processes	No	No	Yes	Yes

Using APEX Region Modals

A fine balance is provided by the APEX region solution. It is possible to render a report with a button that will invoke the modal pop up for a particular record. Once the user is finished, the pop up can be closed and data processed, and then onto the next record—all without submitting the page.

This section modifies the original Employees report page to move the EMPNO and ENAME fields defined in Chapter 8 to reside in a modal region, populated on load and then any changes saved with the click of a button.

Define Modal Region

Edit the Employees report page and create a new HTML region using the template *Inline Dialog*. Set the *Position* to *Inline Dialogs*. Hopefully both are obvious selections and they result in the region appearing as the modal pop up when invoked. Note the Template Options available to dialogs. I set mine to use the small dialog size. Set the *Static ID* to p2_modal. This will be referenced to open the correct dialog.

Now drag and drop the EMPNO and ENAME fields from the Employees report region to the modal region.

Adding a Create Button

There may already be a Create button on the employees report so leave that one to it's existing job of calling the employee page. Duplicate the Create button and then rename the button name and label to MODAL. It set the both to the Edit button position, as to place them in the regiontitle bar. Set both buttons to the Edit position, as to place them in the region's title bar. Set the *Action* to be defined by a dynamic action.

Create Dynamic Action

A JavaScript function has been provided in the theme library that displays the modal dialog on demand. Open the JavaScript console and start typing "open". An autocomplete tip should appear where you can select the function openModal. Figure 12-5 shows the function definition. Chrome allows you click through to see the file where the function is defined in the relevant JavaScript file.

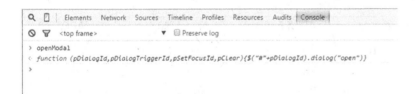

Figure 12-5. *JavaScript function definition for openModal*

Notice how the function is just a wrapper to the .dialog() function. These modals are just a larger version of the dialogs in Chapter 11.

Right-click the Modal button to create a new dynamic action for the Click event. Set the action to execute the JavaScript in Listing 12-1.

Listing 12-1. Invoke the Modal Using JavaScript and Clear Values

```
openModal('p2_modal');
$('#P2_EMPNO').val('').focus(); // this will clear the empno without invoking a change event
$s('P2_ENAME','');              // this will clear the ename using a supplied API
```

There is no need for Selection Type, so clear if prompted. There is also no need to execute on page load. The Modal button is now ready for use.

Modifying Report Button DA

The existing dynamic action for the Report button event can be extended to include a call to openModal() in the JavaScript action. The placement may be before or after the $s() call.

Saving the Data

Now at runtime, an empty modal will be displayed when the Modal button is pressed, or the relevant record displayed when pressing any of the Report buttons. Figure 12-6 shows the modal after a Record button is pressed with the fields populated from the existing process.

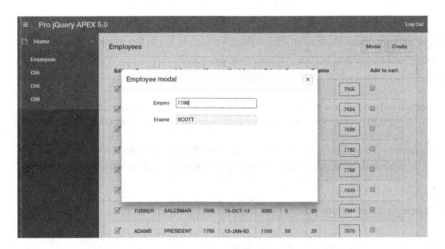

Figure 12-6. *Modal region template in action*

Clicking the cross icon or pressing escape will close the modal. If you want to process any data changes, a Save button is required on the modal region.

Add a hot Save button on the modal region in the Create region position. Set the button action to be defined as dynamic action.

The corresponding dynamic action could execute the PL/SQL necessary to apply the data to the database, remembering to utilize the *Page Items To Submit* property to send information the browser knows to the database. Then another action could refresh the Employees region and another action to notify the user.

Alternatively, all this can be done using a JavaScript action calling an AJAX process, as shown in Listing 12-2. This means the JavaScript does everything required in one place, and subsequent actions conditional on successful update.

Listing 12-2. JavaScript Component of Save Button

```
/* invoke PL/SQL then close/refresh/alert upon return */
apex.server.process
  ("CB_SAVE" // AJAX callback (PL/SQL code)
  ,{ // pData
    pageItems : '#P2_EMPNO,#P2_ENAME'
    }
  ,{ // pOptions
     dataType:"text"
    }
).done(
  function(pData){
    closeModal('p2_modal');
    $('#p2_emps').trigger('apexrefresh');
    alert($v('P2_ENAME')+' saved');
});
```

Unfortunately, you cannot utilize APEX page-processing features with the Save button unless the page is submitted, which defeats the main purpose of this modal template. Any validation of data needs to be done prior to calling the AJAX process.

■ **Note** If the report fails to refresh, check thatEnable Partial Page Refresh is Yes in the region attributes. If still a problem, enable Debug and check that PL/SQL did not raise exception.

The PL/SQL callback needs to handle new or existing records, so a SQL MERGE can handle both scenarios in one statement. The USING component can source information from session state by querying from dual.

The :P2_EMPNO value is matched to existing data in emp table. If it's found, an UPDATE is applied. When no record exists, an INSERT is executed. Note the usage of table aliases to make it clear where data is sourced in the query.

Listing 12-3. PL/SQL Callback for Save Button

```
MERGE INTO emp e
USING (select :P2_EMPNO empno, :P2_ENAME ename from dual) t
ON (e.empno = t.empno)
WHEN MATCHED THEN
  UPDATE SET ename = t.ename
WHEN NOT MATCHED THEN
  INSERT (empno, ename)
  VALUES (t.empno, t.ename);
```

The page is nearly complete. You may notice that after updating a record, the Row button no longer works. This is because the region has been executed, but the click event on the button hasn't been reapplied.

Edit the Row button dynamic action and modify the Event Scope attribute to Dynamic. An optional Static Container attribute will apear, but can improve the performance of the page if supplied. Event Scope should also be updated for the check box dynamic action.

Summary

When it comes to modal forms in APEX, many options are available and each option has strengths and weaknesses. Care needs to be taken when selecting the appropriate solution for your circumstance. A sledgehammer is not required when a basic form will do, but you also need to provide your users with consistency.

APEX version, project size, and developer skill level are all major factors that should influence your decision. Explore them all and see what works best for you.

CHAPTER 13

■ ■ ■

Receiving Information from the Database

The information format to be returned usually takes one of a few forms, the first being basic textual confirmation of an event. The second could be a small, discrete set of output given a specific input. Finally, using JSON as the output format offers great flexibility since its structure is so dynamic. A common uses for JSON-formatted data ranges from bundling a small set of discrete data to passing reportable information from the database to a charting framework such as Google Visualizations.

While discussing processing in Chapter 9, we demonstrated receiving information from the database in both a discrete format plus the heterogeneous JSON format. This chapter will dive deeper into what options are available when sending information from the database to the browser to help you decide which option suits your given situation.

Using htp.prn

A precursor to APEX was called mod_plsql, which was accompanied with the htp and htf packages to produce HTML from PL/SQL. This still goes on under the hood of APEX and any time a dynamic PL/SQL region is defined.

The procedure htp.prn is the mechanism to send information back to the JavaScript that invoked the PL/SQL callback. All the examples used so far include such a call. For instance, this example returns the literal string to calling JavaScript:

```
htp.prn('Hello Universe');
```

The JavaScript in Listing 13-1 makes this value available in the success function via the pData parameter. In this example the data returned is expected in text format, thanks to the dataType parameter.

Listing 13-1. Basic AJAX Call

```
apex.server.process
  ("CB_BASIC"
  ,{ }
  ,{ dataType:"text" }
).done(
  function(pData){
    console.log(pData);
```

```
    // split string into an array
    var results = pData.split(':');
    console.log(results[0]);
    console.log(results[1]);
});
```

This simple yet effective pattern is useful for sending single pieces of information back to the browser. This could be a descriptive value for a code, table attribute based on the provided key, or an indicator of process completion such as PASS or FAIL.

Create a new page in your application with one HTML region. Then create a PL/SQL callback called CB_BASIC that executes the following:

```
htp.prn('ABC');
htp.prn('123');
```

Create a button on the HTML region that will execute the JavaScript in Listing 13-1. Clicking the button will display the following in the browser console window:

```
ABC123
ABC
123
```

Using a small string of text as output has been enough to manage the examples used so far and can be useful for simple validation and user feedback.

Processing Delimited Data

Delimited strings can be a useful way to manage data across many programming languages. One of the most ubiquitous spreadsheet formats (CSV) uses delimiters to separate data within a text file.

The delimited format can be useful when the amount of data is minimal and the code can be kept relatively simple. Some examples have been available since APEX 3.1 that return delimited data in a text string. The first I recall seeing related to cascading LOVs before they were declaratively available in 4.x.

Modify the PL/SQL in the CB_BASIC callback to include a colon as the delimiter. For example:

```
htp.prn('ABC:123');
```

JavaScript provides a function to split strings into constituent components into an array, which is similar to the PL/SQL function apex_util.string_to_table(). Extend the success function in the AJAX call to include the following:

```
var results = pData.split(':'); // split string into an array
console.log(results[0]);
console.log(results[1]);
```

Refresh the page and press the button to see the following output in the console window:

```
ABC:123
ABC
123
```

The delimited result is followed with the individual elements from the generated array. This technique can still be found in APEX plug-ins and scenarios where a fixed amount of values is expected such as success/failure messaging with a supplied reason.

For instance, a PL/SQL block could return success indicator as the first value, and the relevant value or error in the second position:

```
select value
into l_variable
from my_table;

htp.p('SUCCESS:'||l_variable);

exception when no_data_found then
  htp.prn('ERROR:'||sqlerrm);
```

The calling JavaScript can then respond based on this information from the database.

Larger Data Using JSON

JSON is a ubiquitous, lightweight data-interchange format used by many JavaScript libraries, such as those that produce graphical representations of data such as Google Visualizations.

Why Use JSON?

While AJAX was emerging technology, JSON appeared as an alternative to XML and has since become widely adopted as the protocol of choice for data communication.

JSON is a more prominent feature of the 12c database, and APEX 5.0 also sees the release of dedicated APIs on the format to help receive and process JSON from external sources. Generating JSON can be done from Oracle Rest Data Services (ORDS), a dedicated APEX API, or some clever SQL, which can then be consumed by third-party JavaScript libraries included in your page.

A number of examples for using JSON include the following:

- A simple JSON string can replace the need for delimiting data.

- PL/SQL dynamic actions with *Page Items to Return* can be written manually using JavaScript that processes JSON.

- ORDS web services use JSON as a format option.

- Libraries such as Google Visualizations, D3.js, and vis.js accept JSON data formatted to their specification.

JSON is often useful when the data varies in quantity and/or structure. When used by libraries, you typically do not process objects individually but rather pass them as a data set sent to APIs, information such as a set of data points for a chart.

JSON Syntax

JSON format is similar to XML in its structure of nested attribute-value pairs, though differences do exist. JSON is a simpler format designed only for data representation, as shown in the following example:

```
{
  "firstName": "Scott"
 ,"lastName": "Wesley"
 ,"oracleACE": true
 ,"skillset": [
    {
      "tool": "forms",
      "yearStarted": 2000
    },
    {
      "tool": "apex",
      "yearStarted": 2008
    }
  ],
  "retired": null
}
```

JSON objects are surrounded by curly brackets, while JSON arrays also include square brackets. In the example, the object is a person with a number of attributes, including an array of skills.

JSON recognizes basic datatypes of strings, numbers, and booleans, plus the ability to nest further data as an array. There is no specific date format and their interpretation will be dependent on the library consuming it. Nulls are represented with the word *null*.

You may have already encountered JSON when utilizing the `.css()` jQuery function:

```
$("p").css({"background-color": "red", "font-size": "150%"});
```

Here two value pairs are provided that describe the CSS attributes for the selector, surrounded by the curly brackets.

Handling JSON within the AJAX Call

By default, the `apex.server.process` call expects output in JSON format unless the `dataType` parameter specifies otherwise. The PL/SQL callback needs to generate a string in the JSON format, which is then returned to JavaScript and perhaps sent to the relevant framework to render as a chart or specific visualization.

Elements in the JSON output can be referenced in a manner similar to arrays, as seen in Chapter 9 using the following:

```
pData.row[0].ENAME
```

However, the result is often sent as a full data set to the subsequent library. Chapter 14 will demonstrate an example of this in further detail, building a timeline chart with `vis.js`.

Generating JSON

A number of methods are available to produce JSON content. As Figure 13-1 shows, SQL Developer 4.1 allows you to generate JSON content on the fly, but this will not be enough to integrate with APEX and jQuery.

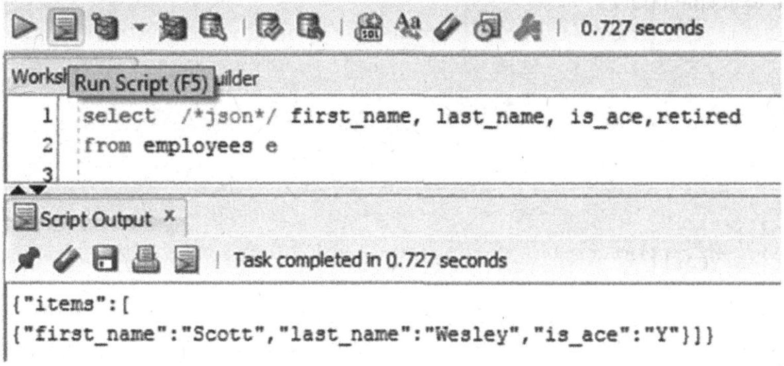

Figure 13-1. *Generate JSON from ad hoc query in SQL Developer*

However, you could use this output to help determine what your code should produce.

Generating JSON Using LISTAGG()

Since information for a JSON data set comes from the database, it's possible to generate the string directly from a SQL statement instead of generating it programmatically in PL/SQL with loops and conditions.

The Oracle database provides a number of dedicated functions for XML such as XMLELEMENT, XMLFOREST, and XMLAGG. All queries needed for JSON is the analytical function LISTAGG(). XML functions can technically achieve the same task, just a lot slower, as shown in Listing 13-2.

Listing 13-2. DDL and DML for LISTAGG Demonstration Tables

```
create table emp_skills
  (emp_id  number not null
  ,tool    varchar2(30) not null
  ,year    number not null
);

create table employees
  (id          number not null
  ,first_name  varchar2(30)
  ,last_name   varchar2(30)
  ,is_ace      varchar2(1)
  ,retired     varchar2(1)
);

insert into employees values (1, 'Scott', 'Wesley', 'Y', null);
insert into emp_skills values (1, 'Forms', 2000);
insert into emp_skills values (1, 'APEX', 2008);
```

Create the tables as defined in Listing 13-2, and then create a new callback CB_LISTAGG using the PL/SQL from Listing 13-3. This generates the same content as shown in the JSON syntax example. A single JSON object is produced with a nested set of skills. The LISTAGG function concatenates records from the skills query in the WITH statement, which is then included in the single main string, as shown in Listing 13-3.

Listing 13-3. PL/SQL to Generate Example JSON

```
/* CB_LISTAGG */
declare
  l_json  varchar2(4000);
begin
with skills as
  (select '{ '
          ||' "tool":"'||s.tool||'"'
          ||',"yearStarted":"'||s.year||'"'
          ||'}' nested_json
       ,s.emp_id
   from emp_skills s)
select '{ '
        ||' "firstName":"'||e.first_name||'"'
        ||',"lastName":"'||e.last_name||'"'
        ||',"OracleACE":"'||nvl2(e.is_ace, 'true', 'false')||'"'
        ||',"skillset":'||(  select '['||listagg( s.nested_json, ',')
                                                  within group (order by null)
                                    ||']' as nested_data
                              from skills s
                              where s.emp_id = e.id
                            )
        ||',"retired":"'||nvl2(e.retired, '"Y"', 'null')||'"'
        ||'} ' json
into    l_json
from    employees e;

htp.p(l_json);
end;
```

Create a new button to invoke this callback using JavaScript in Listing 13-4, similar to the first example.

Listing 13-4. JavaScript Stub to Invoke Callback That Returns JSON Content

```
apex.server.process
  ("CB_LISTAGG"
  ,{ }
  ,{ dataType:"json" }
).done(
  function(pData){
    console.log(pData.emps[0]);
});
```

A common consideration with this method is the size of the string produced and how it's handled within PL/SQL. Despite improvements string sizes in 12c, LISTAGG can still only handle 4,000 characters, while variable length strings in PL/SQL scale to 32,767 characters.

For larger data sets, a custom aggregate function can be defined to output a CLOB use LISTAGG. Carsten Czarski offers this solution at his blog:

```
http://sql-plsql-de.blogspot.com.au/2014/01/sql-listagg-mit-clob-ausgabe-kein.html
```

LISTAGG is fine for smaller data sets. It can also be adopted for CLOBs, as queries written this way can be adapted to handle each row iteratively within a PL/SQL loop.

Oracle RESTful Data Services

While this book focuses on the use of jQuery within APEX, producing JSON is made even simpler with ORDS.

ORDS was formerly known as the Oracle APEX Listener, but now it includes more functionality than just serving as the middle tier between the database and the browser.

If you're using ORDS, you can find a simple tutorial on the topic at Dimitri Gielis' blog:

```
http://dgielis.blogspot.com.au/2015/01/json-for-apex-developers-part-1.html
```

There is also a more extensive Oracle by Example (OBE) at http://www.oracle.com/webfolder/technetwork/tutorials/obe/cloud/dbservice/restfulws/restfulws.html.

The functionality is declarative where you only need to provide a simple SQL statement. JavaScript can request the JSON data with the following call:

```
$.getJSON("https://www.yourdomain.com/ords/module/emp_json/", function(json_data) {
  console.log(json_data);
});
```

Should you find yourself in an environment using ORDS, this solution offers an easy, declarative method for producing JSON content.

Community APIs

Open source libraries aren't limited to JavaScript frameworks. An Oracle PL/SQL library is also available with the codename Alexandria. It can be found at https://code.google.com/p/plsql-utils/.

The suite of libraries includes a package, JSON_UTIL_PKG, which will generate JSON output from the input of a REF CURSOR.

APEX 5.0 and Oracle 12c APIs

Due to the growing uptake of JSON as a communication format between organizations, the latest releases of the Oracle database and APEX include their own APIs for reading and interpreting the data. The JSON_TABLE database function allows JSON data to be queried like a relational view and database tables can be configured for storing JSON text.

The APEX_JSON supplied package provides functions to interrogate properties of a JSON object and write individual elements. This means you don't need to worry about the quantity or placement of brackets as the API handles this. The API could be used to create the elements individually:

```
begin
  apex_json.open_object;

  apex_json.write('firstName', 'Scott');
  apex_json.write('lastName', 'Wesley');
  apex_json.write('oracleACE', true);

  ...

  apex_json.close_object;
end;
```

The write procedure is heavily overloaded and will accept ref cursors. Listing 13-5 shows a query reminiscent of the LISTAGG query producing almost identical JSON, though in this case it encases the result within an emps object.

Listing 13-5. JavaScript Stub to Invoke Callback That Returns JSON Content

```
/* CB_APEX_JSON */
DECLARE
  c sys_refcursor;
BEGIN
  open c for
    select first_name, last_name, is_ace
      ,cursor(select tool
                   ,year
               from emp_skills s
              where s.emp_id = e.id) skills
      ,retired
    from employees e;

  apex_json.open_object;
  apex_json.write('emps', c);
  apex_json.close_object;
END;
```

Feel free to incorporate this as the third example on your page. For this to be interpreted the same as Listing 13-3, the JavaScript can refer to the first emps object using the following:

```
console.log(pData.emps[0])
```

JavaScript APIs

A few functions are available on the JavaScript end that help deal with the JSON format. The most useful I find relates to debugging the output.

It's easy to miss a comma or bracket when first generating JSON to be supplied to a library. The feedback is usually not very informative. A typical error is shown in Figure 13-2.

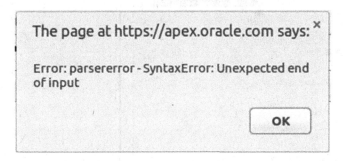

Figure 13-2. *Uninformative JSON error*

The following code will transform the JSON object back into a string in the console window:

```
console.log(JSON.stringify(pData));
```

Alternatively, the generated string could be logged from within the PL/SQL block and then harvested for manual validation.

Conversely, the following JavaScript will transform a properly formatted string into a JSON object:

```
var jsonObj = JSON.parse(jsonStr);
```

Validating JSON

The structure of the JSON format makes it easy to validate. A number of online validators exist to help locate any reported issues with the JSON string.

Figure 13-3 shows the example syntax with an errant comma added. The string is parsed and an error is located and highlighted, much like SQL IDEs help locate errant syntax. While SQL Developer may help ensure all quotes are paired correctly, it will not do the same for JSON formatting.

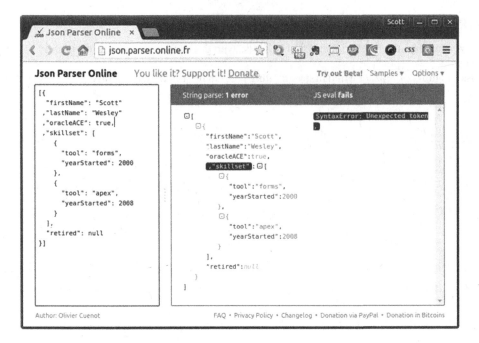

Figure 13-3. *Online JSON parser indicating syntax error*

Modifying the JSON text on the left-hand box will provide immediate feedback on the right. Note this parser requires the JSON object is surrounded by square brackets.

Undocumented APIs

In Chapter 9, I demonstrated a procedure that would output JSON from a supplied string. While this procedure is not formally documented, it was generally regarded as acceptable to use:

```
apex_util.json_from_sql('select * from emp where empno = :P6_EMPNO');
```

```
{"row":[{"EMPNO":7900,"ENAME":"JAMES","JOB":"CLERK","MGR":7698,"HIREDATE":"12\u002F03\
u002F1981","SAL":950,"COMM":"","DEPTNO":30}]}
```

One reason for the lack of documentation is due to the uncertainty of how JSON would be managed in future releases, so these functions were put on hold. Now supplied package apex_json should be able to replace these calls. Another procedure accepts a delimited list of items, and it will build the JSON string from the session state values of those items:

```
apex_util.json_from_items('P6_ENAME');
```

```
{"item":[{"id":"P6_ENAME","value":"KING"}]}
```

Undocumented JavaScript function `json_SetItems` exists to transform the item id/value pairs to the relevant browser items. This provides a simple method of synchronizing values in session state to the associated items in the browser, as opposed to assigning the attributes manually.

Summary

You don't need dedicated APIs to generate JSON content, but the number of JSON-related APIs has grown significantly in the latest Oracle software releases.

The method of generating JSON content will depend on the given situation, and this chapter has outlined a variety of options available to the APEX developer.

The next step in understanding how JSON is used in APEX as a data communication catalyst is to generate a soup-to-nuts example using JSON generated from the database to feed a charting library.

Reporting Options

CHAPTER 14

■ ■ ■

Adding Visualization with JSON

There is a saying, "A picture paints a thousand words." Built-in charting tools in the APEX environment help paint those pictures. Sometimes the built-in libraries don't have the features required to paint particular pictures, so we need to rely on third-party libraries.

The example in this chapter will map the APEX support schedule across versions onto a visual timeline using vis.js. Instructions will guide you through the process of including the library, communicating data from the database to the library using JSON, and then rendering the visualization.

Why Visualizations?

This decade has seen prolific use of *infographics* to present information to an audience. Figure 14-1 shows a chart generated from Google Trends representing the term's use since 2007.

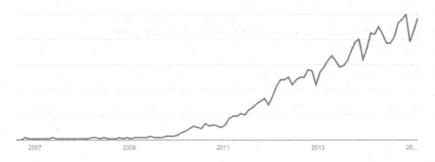

Figure 14-1. *Use of term infographic on the Internet according to Google*

Isn't the picture it tells amazing? Online graphics have been very successful using this visual power to communicate information that deserves a visual point of reference. Demonstrating a sense of scale is a common example, one that webcomic XKCD does particularly well demonstrating the depths of the world's lakes and oceans.

www.xkcd.com/1040/

Infographics need not be static images. Improvements in browser technologies allow infographics to be interactive, such as one demonstrating the scale of the universe by Cary and Michael Huang at htwins.net. I've noticed progressive television news broadcasts use infographics while telling key stories. This method works well because our brains do better at comprehending information that is sensory diverse and more engaging.

Given the right tools, we have a database of information that could be represented visually to communicate information more effectively to the user.

Visualization Libraries

There are a number of third-party JavaScript libraries offering the ability to produce many types of data visualization. Some readers may have seen Roel Hartman include Google Visualizations within APEX applications, namely the organization chart. Figure 14-2 shows another example, the Google Visualization Timeline.

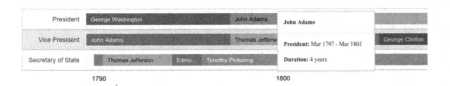

Figure 14-2. *Google Visualization Timeline*

For timeline graphs, I've found the vis.js library more flexible and responsive than the Google Visualization shown in the graphic. The vis output can be zoomed in and out, and the user can drag the chart to move the timeframe. More advanced implementations can update the data based on user interaction.

The vis.js library also has a number of different styles available to choose from, depending on specifically how you need to visualize date data. The example used in this chapter uses the Subgroups format, demonstrated at the following URL:

http://visjs.org/examples/timeline/30_subgroups.html

Each format has a basic example that accompanies further documentation, which makes determining how to format the data even easier.

Preparing Data

To utilize a timeline report, you need date data. Listing 14-1 defines a table that defines the general availability date for each APEX version and its associated end of support date, as provided by Oracle.

Listing 14-1. Define Supporting Table

```
CREATE TABLE apex_timeline
  (version VARCHAR2(10)
  ,ga_date DATE
  ,support_ends DATE
)
/
```

```
-- As sourced from http://www.oracle.com/us/support/library/lifetime-support-technology-069183.pdf
insert into apex_timeline (version,ga_date,support_ends)
        values ('1.6',date '2005-07-01',date '2008-12-01');
insert into apex_timeline (version,ga_date,support_ends)
        values ('2.2',date '2006-08-01',date '2009-08-01');
insert into apex_timeline (version,ga_date,support_ends)
        values ('3.1',date '2008-02-01',date '2011-02-01');
insert into apex_timeline (version,ga_date,support_ends)
        values ('3.2',date '2009-02-01',date '2012-02-01');
insert into apex_timeline (version,ga_date,support_ends)
        values ('4.1',date '2011-08-01',date '2016-08-01');
insert into apex_timeline (version,ga_date,support_ends)
        values ('4.2',date '2012-10-01',date '2017-10-01');
insert into apex_timeline (version,ga_date,support_ends)
        values ('5.0',date '2015-04-01',date '2020-04-01');
```

This format represents data that will be easily consumed by a timeline chart. It is possible to map less normalized data to a timeline, for instance where each record has a number of date columns representing the start/end dates for each timeline entry. The SQL UNPIVOT operation can be used in these cases to transform the data.

Figure 14-3 shows how this information will look when mapped using the vis.js library.

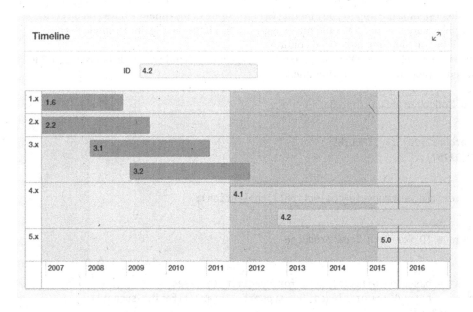

Figure 14-3. *Timeline as rendered by vis.js*

The x-axis represent years over time, and the y-axis categorises major dot point releases. Each event within the chart shows the support boundaries for specific versions. Colours are used to represent status.

Preparing a Page

The page will need a region to house the timeline chart, plus some supporting components to complete the solution.

Create a new page with a static content region. Update the region to include a Static ID of p14_timeline. This should produce a basic DIV definition on the page, which the library will transform into a chart. Alternatively, you can place the following code within your page where you see fit:

```
<div id="p14_timeline"></div>
```

Create a page item P14_ID in the region, which will be used to store which timeline event is clicked, allowing for future extensions beyond the scope of this chapter. A dynamic action can be added on change of the item to respond to a click on the data point, perhaps to open a dialog displaying details of the timeline event.

Page properties will be detailed once other components have been added.

Create Collection

To prepare data for the timeline, a number of passes through the relevant tables is often required. Depending on your data source and level of interaction within the page, you may find it beneficial to page performance to build a collection based on the data on page load. There is a trade-off in doing so, but it's not uncommon to do so when the same data set is used for multiple charts within a page, such as a dashboard.

The apex_timeline table of six rows won't have any issue, but the pattern is worth demonstrating. It will benefit larger examples, opening the opportunity for quicker refreshing of the timeline based on any criteria managed within the page. Larger examples could mean aggregating a large data set into a smaller set of records, or sourcing data from different tables and columns.

To create a collection, define a PL/SQL process to run on page load. Include the code in Listing 14-2 to store data transformed in preparation for the timeline.

Listing 14-2. Create Collection of Data from Base Table

```
declare
  l_collection varchar2(20) :='TIMELINE';
  l_sql varchar2(32767);
begin

  apex_collection.create_or_truncate_collection(l_collection);

  for r_rec in (
   -- define a unique ID for each item produced
    select
      version
     ,ga_date      -- based on official data for specific releases
     ,support_ends -- http://www.oracle.com/us/support/library/lifetime-support-
      technology-069183.pdf
     -- slightly messy way of defining major groups given the basic data
     ,substr(version, 1, 1) group_id
     -- class for group background
     ,case substr(version,1,1)
      when '2' then 'teal'
      when '3' then 'green'
      when '4' then 'blue'
      when '5' then 'apex5'
```

```
      else 'htmldb'
      end group_background
      -- class is used to dress the timeline items
      ,case
       when support_ends < sysdate then 'desupported'
       when version like '5%' then 'ga_future'
       else 'ga_current'
       end item_class
    from apex_timeline t
    order by ga_Date
  ) loop

    apex_collection.add_member
     (p_collection_name => l_collection
     ,p_c001 => r_rec.version
     ,p_c002 => r_rec.group_id
     ,p_c003 => r_rec.group_background
     ,p_c004 => r_rec.item_class
     ,p_d001 => r_rec.ga_date
     ,p_d002 => r_rec.support_ends
     );
    -- consider using create_collection_from_query_b

  end loop;

end populate_collection;
```

This listing will recreate the collection on each load of the page. Frequency of re-creation can be adjusted for larger data sets.

The listing also adds members to the collection one at a time so column datatypes can be referenced explicitly, hence keeping the code concise and reducing length for the book. For performance, it's better to use the apex_collection.create_collection_from_query_b API that builds the collection using bulk operations, which can improve performance of larger data sets.

Comments on the columns in the query help describe their purpose, which will become clearer when utilised in PL/SQL callbacks. When using collections, it can be beneficial to define a view over the collection to help with field mapping.

Create AJAX Callbacks

AJAX callbacks allow communication to and from the database without submitting the page. Google Suggest was an early example of AJAX in action. This ability enables web applications to become more user-friendly by increasing interaction without needing cumbersome page submission.

The vis.js library will render the timeline via a JavaScript call. Prior to this two PL/SQL, callbacks will be invoked, which will generate the JSON data used by the library.

■ **Note**   If your environment uses ORDS, the JSON could be generated via a web service.

You can use the documentation at visjs.org to see further details on how attributes in the JSON data are utilized in the timeline as well as what other attributes are available.

getGroups

The timeline format I've chosen consists of groups of data that appear on the y-axis, along with dated events within the timeline.

The first callback defines a JSON dataset that consists of groups representing the major point releases, such as 3.x and 4.x. Use the code from listing 14-3 to create AJAX callback called getGroups.

Listing 14-3. PL/SQL Callback Returning Groups

```
/* getGroups */
declare
  c sys_refcursor;
begin
  open c for
    select group_id    as "id"
          ,group_id||'.x' as "content"
    from (
      select distinct c002 group_id
      from  apex_collections
      where collection_name = 'TIMELINE'
    );

  apex_json.write(c);
end getGroups;
```

This procedure could use the LISTAGG technique for generating JSON data directly into a string, but it was even simpler to send the SQL to the API.

getItems

Each box to display in the timeline is defined as an item that belongs to one of the defined groups. The definition of subgroups allow the items to be in their own row within each group, as opposed to potentially overlapping each other on the same row.

Create a second AJAX callback called getItems using Listing 14-4.

Listing 14-4. PL/SQL Callback to Return Items

```
/* getItems */
declare
  cursor c_sql is
select '{"id":"'||apex_version||'","group":"'||group_id||'"'
  ||',"content":"'||apex_version||'"'
  ||',"title":"'||apex_version||to_char(date1,' Mon-YY')||to_char(date2,' - Mon-YY')||'"'
  ||',"className":"'||item_class||'"'
  ||',"subgroup":"'||apex_version||'"'
  ||',"subgroupOrder":"'||rn||'"'
  ||',"release":'||'"'||apex_version||'"'
  ||',"start":'||'"'||to_char(date1,'"yyyy"-"mm"-"dd"')||'"'
  ||',"end":"'||to_char(date2,'"yyyy"-"mm"-"dd"')||'"}'
    AS json
```

```
from (
  select n001 id
        ,c001 apex_version
        ,c002 group_id
        ,d001 date1 -- GA date
        ,d002 date2 -- support ends
        ,c004 item_class
         -- order the items chronologically
        ,row_number() over (order by d001 desc) rn
  from   apex_collections
  where collection_name = 'TIMELINE'
)
where date1 is not null;

  type t_data  is table of c_sql%rowtype index by pls_integer;
  l_data    t_data;
  l_background  varchar2(2000);

begin
  -- Could not combine results with apex_json
  -- so building the string piecemeal
  sys.htp.prn('['); -- open the json string

  -- start by producing individual items to be shown in timeline
  open c_sql;
  loop
    -- process data in chunks, optimal limit size varies
    fetch c_sql bulk collect into l_data limit 10;

    for i in 1..l_data.count loop
      -- each json object separated by comma.
      sys.htp.prn(l_data(i).json||',');
    end loop;

    exit when c_sql%notfound;
  end loop c_sql;
  close c_sql;

  -- No need to trim final comma before output since
  -- a second set of json objects are being added.
  -- These represent the coloured backgrounds for the various eras of APEX

  -- The data set is small so listagg() ok
  select listagg('{"id":"background_'||apex_version||'"' -- IDs can be alphanumeric
    ||',"type":"background"'
    ||',"className":"'||group_background||'"'
    ||',"start":'||''''||to_char(date1,'""yyyy"-"mm"-"dd""')||''''
    ||',"end":"'||to_char(date2,'""yyyy"-"mm"-"dd""')||'"}'
      ,',') within group (order by date1)  json
  into l_background
  from (
```

```
select c002 group_id
       ,c001 apex_version
       ,d001 date1
       -- use the end date or the next start date, whatever started first
       ,least(d002, nvl(lead(d001) over (order by c002), d002)) date2
       ,c003 group_background
  from  apex_collections
  where collection_name = 'TIMELINE'
);

  -- since JSON string in one variable it can be trimmed during output
  sys.htp.prn(rtrim(l_background,',')||']'); -- include closing square bracket

end getItems;
```

This procedure actually produces two sets of JSON objects. The first are the items in the timeline and they are generated iteratively within a PL/SQL loop. Bulk processing has been added to demonstrate how larger data sets could be processed more efficiently.

The second data set represents the background periods of time with a class to define its color. It also uses LISTAGG to aggregate the data, and makes trimming the final comma simpler. APEX_JSON could not be used in this case as the two queries could not be combined, nor would successive calls to the write() procedure form the JSON required by the timeline library.

Page Properties

To complete the process you need to include the vis library in the page then invoke JavaScript on page load. Also required are the classes utilized in the data to colour chart components.

Including vis Library

Edit page properties and add thefollowing URLs in the respective JavaScript and CSS File URL attributes:

```
//cdnjs.cloudflare.com/ajax/libs/vis/4.8.2/vis#MIN#.js
```

and

```
//cdnjs.cloudflare.com/ajax/libs/vis/4.8.2/vis#MIN#.css
```

The files are included via a shared Code Delivery Network (CDN) and the relative URL location is used to leave the browser to decide which HTTP protocol to use. The inclusion of #MIN# means when running the application in debug mode, the non-minified version will be used.

Dressing the Chart

Add Listing 14-5 as the Inline CSS for the page.

Listing 14-5. CSS to Set Background Colors

```
/* timeline items */
#p14_timeline div.vis-group div.vis-item.desupported {background-color:#F49AA1;}
#p14_timeline div.vis-group div.vis-item.ga_current {background-color:#9AF49F;}
#p14_timeline div.vis-group div.vis-item.ga_future {background-color:#F1F49A;}
/* background eras */
#p14_timeline div.vis-group div.vis-item.htmldb {background-color:lavenderblush;}
#p14_timeline div.vis-group div.vis-item.teal {background-color:#B6FACC;}
#p14_timeline div.vis-group div.vis-item.green {background-color:#D4F7CE;}
#p14_timeline div.vis-group div.vis-item.blue {background-color:#b9d6fc;}
/* JoelK says white represents APEX5, but that doesn't work well in this demo ;p */
#p14_timeline div.vis-group div.vis-item.apex5 {background-color:#D4E4F9;}
```

These classes will add background color to the items and background objects specified in the JSON className attribute.

Render the Chart

Copy Listing 14-6 into the Function and Global Variable Declaration page attribute. There is a lot going on in this block of code, but ultimately both PL/SQL callbacks are invoked, and the JSON responses are made available to the charting engine to draw the chart.

The points of complexity with this logic mostly lie with the rendering of the chart being dependent on the return of two AJAX calls. It's easy to respond to only one AJAX event by using the .done() deferred function, but in this case we use .then() to build a dependency chain.

This could be mitigated by generating the JSON as part of the page render, perhaps as a computed page item. However the method used below provides an opportunity to demonstrate more jQuery features.

Further concepts will be summarised below the code, but I've included plenty of inline comments since this provides the best context. I've also included some extra error handling since there are a few moving parts in this chapter that could go wrong. More on debugging in a later section.

Listing 14-6. JavaScript Executed on Page Load

```
/* Define namespace to group related functions */
var p14_timeline = {

init: function() {
  // Display a spinner to show loading in progress
  lSpinner$ = apex.util.showSpinner( $( "#p14_timeline" ) );

  this.getGroups(); // 'this' namespace, the function within it
  // then getItems
  // then drawChart
}

// Get group information from the database
,getGroups: function() {
  apex.debug('fetch group list from DB');
  apex.server.process("getGroups") // name of AJAX callback in APEX page
    .done( // what happens on success
      function(pGroups) { // data returned from PL/SQL
        apex.debug('Number of groups: '+pGroups.length);
```

```
      // output shown in Figure 14-4
      apex.debug(pGroups);
      apex.debug(JSON.stringify(pGroups));

      // convert JSON object returned from PL/SQL into vis data set
      groupSet = new vis.DataSet(pGroups);
   }
  ).then(p14_timeline.getItems) // what happens next in the chain.
   .fail( // what happens if there is some form of failure?
     function( jqXHR, textStatus, errorThrown ) { // parameters sent from framework
       p14_timeline.logFailure('getGroups', jqXHR, errorThrown);
     });
}

// Get item information from the database
,getItems: function() {
  apex.debug('fetch item list from db');
  apex.server.process("getItems"
  ).then( // callbacks: first parameter success, second parameter failure
    function(pItems) {
      apex.debug('Number of items: '+pItems.length);
      apex.debug(pItems);
      // convert JSON to vis object
      itemSet = new vis.DataSet(pItems);

      // now render the chart since both data sets returned
      p14_timeline.drawChart();
    }
    , // what happens if there is some form of failure?
      function( jqXHR, textStatus, errorThrown ) {
        p14_timeline.logFailure('getItems', jqXHR, textStatus, errorThrown);
    }); // end then
}

// only attempt to draw chart once both methods to fetch data are completed
,drawChart: function() {

  // if any errors encountered, don't bother attempting to render chart
  if (p14_timeline.errorCnt != 0) {
    console.log('error:'+p14_timeline.errorCnt);
  }
  else {
    // good to go, let's render the chart
    apex.debug('create visualisation');

    // Further details avialable here
    // http://visjs.org/docs/timeline/#Configuration_Options
    var options = {
      editable: false // for another day
     ,min : new Date(2004, 1, 1) // bound the timeline display
     ,max : new Date(2017, 1, 1)
```

```
        ,zoomMin: 1000 * 60 * 60 * 24 * 31 * 12 *2      // about 2 years in milliseconds, depends
                                                         on chart pixel size
        ,zoomMax: 1000 * 60 * 60 * 24 * 31 * 12 *10     // about 10 years in milliseconds
        ,zoomable : true
        //,moveable : false                             // helps scrolling issues in large charts
        ,maxHeight : "1000px"
        ,stack : false
        ,dataAttributes: ['release']                    // extra data attribute can be handy
    };

    apex.debug('do actual render, with data gathered from db');
    // identifies #p14_timeline div the native way, which returns the single entity, not an
    array like $() does
    var timeline = new vis.Timeline(document.getElementById('p14_timeline'));
    timeline.setOptions(options);
    timeline.setGroups(groupSet);
    timeline.setItems(itemSet);

    // Spinner can be removed now
    lSpinner$.remove();

    // set item when user clicks on timeline entry
    timeline.on('select', function (params) {
      $s('P14_ID', params.items[0]);
    });

  } // end if (errors)

} // end draw chart

// count any errors encountered, like a persistent variable in a package
,errorCnt : 0

// some sort of error encountered
,logFailure: function(pProc, jqXHR, errorThrown ) {
  // information helpful to debugging issue:
  console.log(pProc+' failure');
  console.log(jqXHR.responseText);
  console.log(errorThrown);

  // increment the count the old fashioned way
  this.errorCnt++;

  // the chart isn't going to render now, so update the region
  $('#p14_timeline div.t-Region-body').text('The chart failed to render.');
  // Remove spinner if error raised
  lSpinner$.remove();
}

} // end namespace
```

Set the Execute When Page Loads property to call the defined function:

```
// Initiate the processes to draw chart
p14_timeline.init();
```

Note how the init() function is invoked. It looks just like the dot notation used when invoking procedures in PL/SQL packages. When will the parallels ever cease? In this case the p14_timeline JavaScript namespace prefixes the function.

Namespaces are a way to organise your JavaScript code into a logical hierarchy, very similar to how PL/SQL packages organise procedures and functions. Unfortunately it's a diverse topic with plenty of implementation variety, too much to cover in this book integrating jQuery with APEX.

However, in this case using a namespace was appropriate to group these methods served a worthy demonstration, particularly since the vis.js library utilises a timespace namespace. In Listing 15-6, the namespace is defined in the first line of the code, and functions are defined slightly differently within the code.

The init() function invoked on page load initiates the first process in the chain that ends with vis.Timeline() turning the empty #p14_timeline div into a chart populated with JSON data. Before doing so it renders a spinner to indicate loading status to the user.

The first process initiated gets the list of groups that form the x-axis. Upon completion of the PL/SQL, the .done() function calls vis.DataSet() to convert the returned JSON dataset into the an object type expected by the vis.js library.

The getGroups() function also includes two other deferred event definitions, also referred to as Promises. Once the getGroups function completes, then() promises to execute getItems(). If something goes wrong, fail() will execute in lieu of done().

The getItems() function repeats the decision making process, though the JavaScript is defined differently, again demonstrating the variety of ways the same logic can be syntactically applied. One formal definition of then() is simply

```
deferred.then( doneCallbacks, failCallbacks )
```

You could almost liken it to the difference between named parameters and positional notation in PL/SQL, the only difference is readability. In both cases the fail callback echoes some information to the browser console and increments a counter.

Before attempting to render the chart the final drawChart() method first checks the counter to determine if any errors were encountered while fetching the JSON data. If all clear, some chart options are set to configure the report, of which further details are available in the vis.js documentation.

Finally the empty div is converted to a timeline object, with the options and chart data added in calls to the timeline namespace supplied by the vis.js library. The final act adds an event listener to populate the P14_ID with the ID of the selected timeline entry.

Now run the page to see the timeline in action. Hover your mouse and scroll in/out to change the zoom. Click and drag left and right to slide the window of time displayed.

Handling Bugs

Rarely does code like this come together the first time without some sort of syntax error, particularly when attempting to format JSON data as a string. It can be easy to miss a comma or bracket that won't be picked up by the PL/SQL compiler, or maybe the PL/SQL raised an exception.

When all is going well, the output from the instrumentation of pGroups would like Figure 14-4, outputting the JSON in native format plus the stringified version.

```
▼ [Object, Object, Object, Object, Object] 🗐
  ▼ 0: Object
      content: "1.x"
      id: "1"
    ▶ __proto__: Object
  ▶ 1: Object
  ▶ 2: Object
  ▶ 3: Object
  ▶ 4: Object
    length: 5
  ▶ __proto__: Array[0]
[{"id":"1","content":"1.x"},{"id":"3","content":"3.x"},{"id":"5","content":"5.x"},{"id":"2","content":"2.x"},{"id":"4","content":"4.x"}]
```

Figure 14-4. *Output of correctly formatted JSON*

However, different symptoms appear when something goes wrong. The code already listens for these errors and informs the user, now the developer needs the tools to resolve the issue.

PL/SQL Errors

To illustrate the outcome, raise a contrived exception to the getGroups AJAX Callback by adding the following just after the begin.

```
raise_application_error(-20001,'This could be any exception'); -- add error
```

Save and refresh the timeline page to see the how the error manifests in your particular browser.

Exceptions raised in PL/SQL get added to the function output, thereby rendering the AJAX call a failure as it does not form a valid JSON string. The fail() method executes, logging the output to the browser. The code stops executing before attempting to getItems.

```
getGroups failure
sqlerrm:ORA-20001: This could be any exception
SyntaxError: Unexpected token s
    at Object.parse (native)
    at n.parseJSON (https://apex.oracle.com/i/libraries/jquery/2.1.3/jquery-2.1.3.min.js?
    v=5.0.2.00.07:4:5309)
    at uc (https://apex.oracle.com/i/libraries/jquery/2.1.3/jquery-2.1.3.min.js?
    v=5.0.2.00.07:4:7333)
    at x (https://apex.oracle.com/i/libraries/jquery/2.1.3/jquery-2.1.3.min.js?
    v=5.0.2.00.07:4:10747)
    at XMLHttpRequest.n.ajaxTransport.k.cors.a.crossDomain.send.b (https://apex.oracle.com/
    i/libraries/jquery/2.1.3/jquery-2.1.3.min.js?v=5.0.2.00.07:4:14577)
```

I've included the most pertinent information in the output. The jqXHR.responseText attribute constitutes what would normally become the output. The error message in this case only includes the error text since it was the first thing to happen, but it may include data already streamed.

The syntax error is raised by JavaScript while attempting to parse the output, complaining about the first character in the return string, which should be a bracket.

JSON format errors

Remove the error you added and open the getItems AJAX Callback, then add the following as the penultimate line, just before the end getItems;.

```
sys.htp.prn(']'); -- add error
```

This will add an extra bracket to the JSON output, rendering it invalid. Figure 14-5 shows the output received in the browser console from this JSON error.

Figure 14-5. *Result of JSON error in AJAX call*

The JSON string outputted as the response can be pasted into a JSON parser, many of which are available for free online such as this URL that was mentioned in the previous chapter:

http://json.parser.online.fr

In this case the parser reports the error:

SyntaxError: Unexpected token]

The parser will also help identify where syntax errors are located in the JSON string, as shown in Figure 14-6.

Figure 14-6. *JSON validator highlighting location of syntax error*

The ability to debug and diagnose in this manner is a great supplement to the alternatives. You can run the relevant queries in SQL Developer to help verify output but that doesn't take into account brackets and commas managed by any surrounding PL/SQL.

You can run the callback PL/SQL in SQL Workshop to see the generated JSON, but you will need to amend the code to select from the base table instead of the collection. Otherwise, there will be no results as the collection is available only to your APEX runtime session.

Other errors you may encounter include the following:

```
Invalid start "NaN"
```

This is from the vis library itself, complaining that records with no start date have been included in the data set.

Summary

Oracle APEX offers a number of built-in visualisation options with AnyChart libraries, and from APEX 5.1 we are likely to see Oracle JavaScript Extension Toolkit (JET) incorporated as the primary charting engine. If none of these suit your requirement, the Internet is full of visualization libraries, many of which can be included in your APEX applications with only a few moving parts.

Data is extracted from the database and sent to the chart-rendering framework, but not transmitted online. APEX provides features to furnish data in a variety of ways. This chapter demonstrated how you could piece these components together for your own projects. The same techniques can be adopted for other charting libraries.

■ ■ ■

Applying jQuery Post Render

APEX is a rapid development tool that facilitates quick production of many reports. This part of the book continues to explore options for embellishing these reports, thanks to useful jQuery patterns.

Interactive reports are even more attractive in APEX 5.0, but they aren't the panacea for all problems. Classic reports offer simple yet flexible options for delivering data. This chapter explores three common examples that extend a simple classic report to give your users an impression of a more polished application.

The first example will customize the "no data found" message, the second will highlight cells containing certain data, and the third will add some sparkle to the report totals.

Check Static Region ID

As with most jQuery examples, it's beneficial to isolate the region in question by using a static region ID instead of the surrogate region ID from the APEX metadata.

If you're working through the examples in this book, you've probably already assigned a static ID to the employee list region. Figure 15-1 shows the attribute in the region properties. You may need to show all attributes to see it.

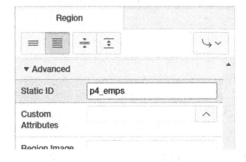

Figure 15-1. *Static ID on the Employee List region*

This enables you to be more specific with jQuery selectors, allowing the browser to only search for elements within a certain region of the page, thus helping performance.

Customize "No Data Found" Message

The default message shown on reports with no rows returned is a drab "no data found." Figure 15-2 shows the output from the page from Chapter 5 where dynamic actions drove search criteria. Not only is it possible to add gloss to this display, the message can be customized at runtime to match entered criteria giving the user a more informed experience.

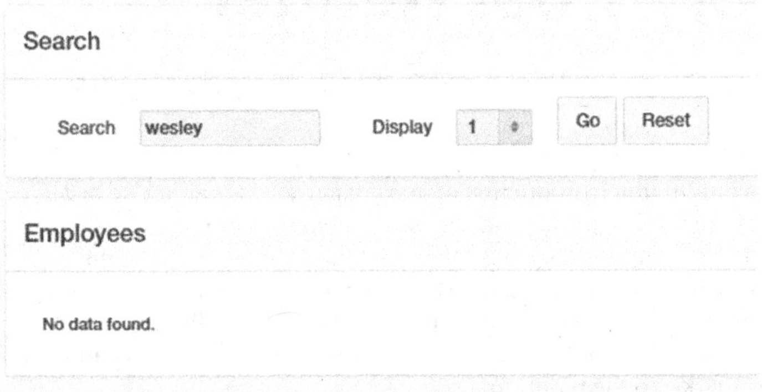

Figure 15-2. Standard "no data found" message

CSS will be used to visually enhance the message, and jQuery will be applied any time the report is rendered to change the text.

Include CSS Style

Place listing 15-1 in the Inline CSS page attribute, which will render a shaded box around the text and make the text more prominent.

Listing 15-1. CSS to Dress the "No Data Found" Message

```
/* Add jazz to the no data found message */
span.nodatafound {
  font-size:120%;
  font-weight: bold;
  border: 1px solid #FC0;
  background: #FFC;
  display: block;
  margin: 2px auto 14px;
  padding: 15px;
  text-align: left;
}
```

Depending on the theme being used and where your CSS is located, you may need to include the !important tag on certain attributes. Figure 15-3 shows how Theme 25 has overwritten attributes such as font styling.

Figure 15-3. *CSS precedence in action*

Without the important clause, the font styles and padding have been superseded by the more specific attributes from 4.2.css.

Extend Dynamic Action

Add a JavaScript action to the dynamic action that refreshes the report.

Back in your application, modify the refresh report dynamic action on the search item and add a JavaScript event after the refresh event that executes the following:

```
$('span.nodatafound').html('No rows found using criteria "'+$v('P4_REPORT_SEARCH')+'"');
```

Note double quotes are used within the outputted text, while single quotes delimit the literal string in the jQuery command.

However, there is a problem with adding JavaScript to this dynamic action. Even though the action sequence might show the Refresh action occurring before the JavaScript, it's probable the refresh will take longer to complete and will overwrite the custom message when the partial page refresh of the report is completed.

The JavaScript needs to be in a dedicated dynamic action using the After Refresh framework event, or be included using your own jQuery.

Using jQuery after Refresh

Remove the JavaScript action you just added and replace functionality by including Listing 15-2 in the Execute When Page Loads page attribute. If records are returned, the jQuery selector will return nothing, hence no span is present to update.

Listing 15-2. Update "No Data Found" Message after Partial Page Refresh

```
// update no data found message after PPR of region
$('#p4_emps').on('apexafterrefresh', function() {
  $(this).find('span.nodatafound')
         .html('No rows found using criteria "'+$v('P4_REPORT_SEARCH')+'"');
});
```

The apexafterrefresh is an event defined by the APEX libraries that will be triggered after the refresh of the given region ID. When triggered, it executes the inline function defined as the second parameter. The final output when searching for a name that doesn't exist will look something like Figure 15-4.

Search

| Search | wesley | Display | 1 ▼ | Go | Reset |

Employees

No rows found using criteria "wesley"

Figure 15-4. No data found with contextual message

Customizing Report Totals

When using the declarative option to add report totals to classic reports, the output prior to APEX 5.0 looked a little unprofessional, as shown in Figure 15-5.

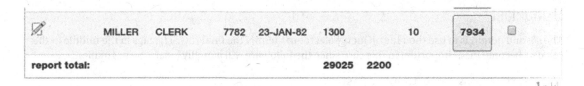

✎	MILLER	CLERK	7782	23-JAN-82	1300		10	7934 ☐
report total:					29025	2200		

1 - 14

Figure 15-5. *Report total in APEX 4.2*

This output was improved in APEX 5.0 by capitalizing the "report total:" text; however, perhaps a requirement is to italicize the totals rows and set the font red.

Add Report Totals

To include totals for Sal and Comm columns, set the Compute Sum attribute to "yes" for both columns.

■ **Tip** This declarative method should suffice for most reports, though ROLLUP can be added to the SQL statement group by clause as an alternative. Doing so will change the required jQuery selectors.

Identifying Page Components

Identifying the final row can be done using a number of techniques. The three demonstrated below get easier each time, but they demonstrate a few options that might be useful in the future.

Using :contains

The first option is to use the :contains selector to locate one of the cells using the text in the first column. The selector is case sensitive, so care needs to be taken regarding APEX version. In APEX 5.0, the contains selector should be 'initcap'.

```
$('#report_p4_emps table tbody tr td:contains("Report Total")')
```

The most important element of this selector in regard to browser performance is the starting ID restricting DOM set to just the one report region named report_p4_emps. Then the selector examines each table cell in that region looking for the provided text.

Since the selector identifies just the specific cell, chained jQuery functions need to be added to select all cells from the totals row.

```
$('#report_p4_emps table tbody tr td:contains("Report Total")')
   .closest('tr').children().css({'font-style':'italic', 'color':'red'})
```

The first function locates the closest row for the given selector. Now that a component of the total row is identified, we can find all its siblings.

The second function identifies all elements one level down in the DOM, hence all the sibling table cells.

The final function applies the CSS necessary for each of these cells and sets the font italic and red, accepting those parameters as a JSON string.

Using :last

The second option is to use the :last jQuery selector to identify the final row. The tags in the middle of the selector become more important in this case since the following will actually locate the pagination:

```
$('#report_p4_emps table tbody tr:last td')
```

The Universal Theme 42 in APEX 5.0 would use the following selector:

```
$('#report_p4_emps table.t-Report-report tbody tr:last td')
  .css({'font-style':'italic', 'color':'red'})
```

In Theme 25, it is possible to use the class .uReport instead. The CSS function would still add the style as per the previous example.

Using CSS

Just because two jQuery solutions are effective doesn't mean you need to use jQuery. There is a purely CSS substitute that will make the browser more efficient in rendering the text as desired. Listing 15-3 shows *Inline CSS* for the page that will identify the last row using the CSS3 selector :last_child, which is equivalent to the :last jQuery selector.

Listing 15-3. CSS Solution Trumps jQuery

```
/* Change font settings for totals row */
#report_p4_emps table.t-Report-report tbody tr:last-child td {
  font-weight : italic;
  color : red;
}
```

Highlighting Cell Backgrounds

Every good Oracle developer knows that generally the more processing that can fit into the SQL, the better. APEX provides conduits for extra styling by allowing HTML expressions within report column definition, allowing conditional formatting based on query content. jQuery offers extra flexibility and conditional rendering options after the page is loaded or report refreshed.

This example will highlight all salaries of at least 3000.

Identifying Report Cells

Identifying cells to highlight is very similar to the report totals example. First, the relevant region is identified and then cells within that region. APEX 5.0 offers particularly granular classes within the templates, so we can specify just the data cells with the .t-Report-cell class.

Certain columns can be identified by locating cells with attributes of a certain value. In this case, it's the column alias defined in the SQL. The following jQuery returns all cells in that column, including the totals row:

```
$('#p4_emps td.t-Report-cell[headers="SAL"]')
```

Utilise the :not operator to exclude the last cell in the set, which is the totals row:

```
$('#p4_emps td.t-Report-cell[headers="SAL"]:not(:last)')
```

Identifying Cells with Certain Values

The value within each DOM element returned can be tested as an integer to determine if the containing cell needs to be highlighted.

Process each array element returned with the jQuery selector using the .each function and convert the text of the cell to an integer before comparing to a numerical amount. $(this) is used to refer to each element iterated, and it can also be referenced when applying the CSS function.

The following code locates the relevant cell elements in the report and then converts each text content to an integer and locates any cells with value greater than or equal to 3000. It then applies a light green background to any that match these criteria:

```
/* Highlight all salary values, excluding totals row */
$('#p2_emps td.t-Report-cell[headers="SAL"]:not(:last)').each(function(){
    if (parseInt($(this).text()) >= 3000)
        $(this).css({"background-color":"lightgreen"});
});
```

This code could be added to an after refresh dynamic action, with Fire on Page Load set to "yes." However, since this is a book about using jQuery in APEX, I'll also demonstrate how to do this manually.

Applying Highlight after Refresh

Since the region can be refreshed without submitting the page, the jQuery to highlight cells needs to be executed after each refresh of the region and apply on page load.

Listing 15-4 incorporates the "no data found" example above with the cell highlighting into one function. This code is defined in the Function and Global Variable Declaration attribute.

Listing 15-4. Code Executed after Refresh of Region

```
function p2_emps_afterrefresh() {

    // update no data found message after PPR of region
    $('#p2_emps span.nodatafound').html('No rows found using criteria "'+$v('P2_REPORT_SEARCH')+'"');

    // Highlight all salary values, excluding totals row
    $('#p2_emps td.t-Report-cell[headers="SAL"]:not(:last)').each(function(){
        if (parseInt($(this).text()) >= 3000)
            $(this).css({"background-color":"lightgreen"});
    });
}
```

The function becomes the handler callback function as per Listing 15-5 to be used in Execute when Page Loads. Not only does it bind the function to after refresh of the region, but it also primes the set of results returned during page render.

Listing 15-5. Code Executed on Page Load

```
// Prime report region
p4_emps_afterrefresh();
// Bind to PPR
$('#p4_emps').on('apexafterrefresh', p4_emps_afterrefresh);
```

The final output combining report total and cell highlighting will look like Figure 15-6, all applied automatically after refreshing the region by typing the letter "d" in the search field.

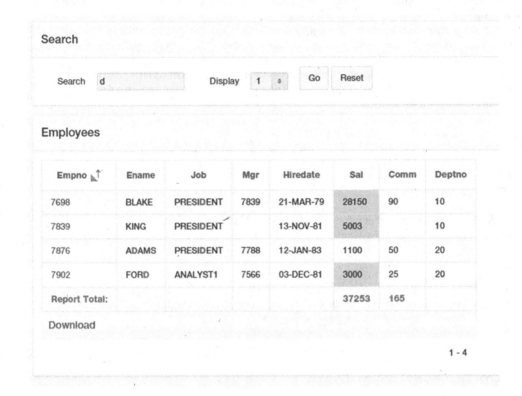

Figure 15-6. *Final outcome of post rendering*

The "d" is highlighted because the region wizard applied &P4_REPORT_SEARCH. to the Highlight Words column attribute, which highlights any content in the cell that matches the provided item.

Summary

While the examples in this chapter are useful in their own right, the coding patterns offer a variety of uses. How you apply these techniques to your own projects is up to you and your creativity.

Finding the balance between including JavaScript in dynamic actions versus including your own jQuery will depend on the page and the project. Be aware that both options exist and each will have their own advantages given the circumstances.

CHAPTER 16

■ ■ ■

Clicking Entire Rows

During my involvement in developing an APEX application for a 10-inch tablet, one of my first observations was the need to expand what areas responded to "clicks." The application was designed to run on either a desktop or tablet, but at the very least it had to be suitable for people selecting options with their fingers.

Our clients were construction workers and had big fingers, so action buttons on each row started to get replaced by the ability to tap (or click) anywhere in the row of a list of records. The response would be to navigate to the next page.

This chapter explores two methods of achieving this goal, once again showing that the development world offers many ways to solve a given problem regardless of the technology.

Method A—Proactive

A blog post from Alex Nuijten inspired this method, which involves defining the given URL for each row, just like you would a button, but then reassigning that link to a click event on the row.

The same employee search page as in Chapter 15 will be modified to navigate to the edit employee page when the user taps on the row. This way the features previously added to the original employee list are not disrupted.

The destination URL could be garnered from an Edit link, which could then be hidden. However, this solution will generate the URL within the SQL.

This method will give an opportunity to demonstrate a simple but vital difference in the way URLs are built from SQL statements. It's a common task, so it's important you don't impact the performance of your application by flooding the SQL Shared Pool with the SQL statement, only differing by session ID.

Taking Care of Performance

Modify the SQL in the employee list to include the API call to generate the URL, as shown in Listing 16-1. Also include a comment hint at the start of the SQL to make it easier to identify later.

Listing 16-1. Modified Start of Employee List SQL

```
select /*+ qb_name(bad_sql) */
apex_util.prepare_url('f?p=&APP_ID.:3:&APP_SESSION.:::::P3_EMPNO:'||empno) as lnk
,empno -- and the rest of your columns in the existing query...
```

This example uses the substitution string syntax to refer to both application ID and session. It's the latter that will impact scalability of your application. To demonstrate, run the page in a number of different sessions. Log out and log in again a few times, running the page each time.

If you leave the column shown in the report, you'll see that each time the session ID is different:

```
f?p=1234:3:34876883201315::::P_EMPNO:7839
```

This is expected and required, but if you take a look at the shared pool, you'll also find the statement appears a number of times.

Now adjust the URL to use a bind variable for the session ID:

```
select /*+ qb_name(good_sql) */
apex_util.prepare_url('f?p=&APP_ID.:3:'||:APP_SESSION||'::::P3_EMPNO:'||empno) as lnk
,empno -- and the rest of your columns...
```

After refreshing the page five times each across three separate sessions, run the query from Listing 16-2. The user will require DBA privileges to select from v$sqlarea, which represents the unique SQL statements found in the shared pool. Since I can't run this statement from apex.oracle.com, the output in Figure 16-1 was from a local instance, hence the different application and page numbers.

Listing 16-2. SQL Statements from the Shared Pool

```
select executions, substr(sql_text,122) sql_text
from sys.v$sqlarea
where sql_text like 'select%qb_name(%sql)%'
and module like '%APEX:APP 113%'
order by last_load_time
```

Note you'll need to modify the where clause to suit how you've written your query, and modify the module to reference your application ID. I've also modified the sql_text column to make the screenshot fit nicely.

Figure 16-1 shows the list of queries found in the shared pool. Note the bad_sql query has three separate entries, at least one for each session. Imagine this amplified with 100 users, compared to the good_sql example where all five executions of the page used the same query.

```
EXECUTIONS   SQL_TEXT
         1   select /*+ qb_name(bad_sql) */  apex_util.prepare_url('f?p=113:2:15576866760066::::P2_EMPNO:'|
         2   select /*+ qb_name(bad_sql) */  apex_util.prepare_url('f?p=113:2:11205215603042::::P2_EMPNO:'|
         2   select /*+ qb_name(bad_sql) */  apex_util.prepare_url('f?p=113:2:5446688828440::::P2_EMPNO:'||
         5   select /*+ qb_name(good_sql) */ apex_util.prepare_url('f?p=113:2:'||:APP_SESSION||'::::P2_EMPN
```

Figure 16-1. Shared pool results

The good_sql method drastically reduces the amount of hard parsing required by the database, which is a very good thing for performance. As a general rule, avoid using the ampersand substitution syntax in SQL and stick with bind variables. Care should also be taken with the user of v() and nv() function, which often should be contained within scalar subqueries.

Add Column

Retain the column from the good_sql example and hide the column in the report. The link column can also be hidden since it will be replaced by the row click.

Add Expression to Report Column

The defined URL still needs to be included within the generated HTML so jQuery can refer to the value and bind to a modified click event.

A number of methods exist to accomplish this, but the most painless is to select an untouched column such as MGR and add a HTML expression, remembering to include the column's data. The hash tags allow substitution of data from the query into the expression that formulates HTML content:

```
#MGR#<a href="#LNK#" class="rowlink" data-id="#EMPNO#" />
```

In some cases, a column may already use a HTML expression that can just be extended with the anchor. The anchor won't be visible to the user, but will be located by a jQuery selector as the destination for the row click event.

The empno is made available as a custom data attribute. This can make it easier to determine the relevant ID compared to searching for content in another column within the row. It's not used in this particular example, but it is a reminder how useful data can be made readily accessible to the event.

Define jQuery Function

jQuery in this example will locate the URL in the report row and reassign the link to the entire table row tag.

First, define a function in the page Function and Global Declaration attribute, as shown in Listing 16-3.

Listing 16-3. Function to Reallocate URL

```
function enable_row_link(p_identifier) {
  // Convert the entire table row to be an anchor
  // <a class="rowlink" href="#THE_URL#"
  // add data="#ID" if you want to make extra information available
  // call: enable_row_click('a.rowlink');
  $(p_identifier).each(function(index) {
    lnk = $(this).attr('href');
    $(this).closest('tr')
     .data('href', lnk)
     .click(function(){
       window.location=$(this).data('href');
     })
     .mouseover(function(){
       $(this).css('cursor', 'pointer');
     })
     .mouseleave(function(){
       $(this).css('cursor', 'default');
     })
  });
}
```

The function will take the identifier of the URL as described in the comments. It will iterate through each element and firstly extract the URL from the anchor.

Next, the function locates the closest TR element, ready for modification via a set of chained functions. It reassigns the URL as a data element to the TR and defines a click event to set the window location to the relevant URL.

As a bonus, the mouse events are added to change the cursor in desktop environments as the mouse hovers over the rows.

Invoke Function

Modify the after refresh function to also include the following:

```
enable_row_link('#p4_emps a.rowlink');
```

Run the page and then hover your mouse over one of the rows. The mouse will change into the pointer, and clicking will open the employee form.

Use Inspect Element to check the table row. Figure 16-2 neatly shows the three event listeners added to the table row.

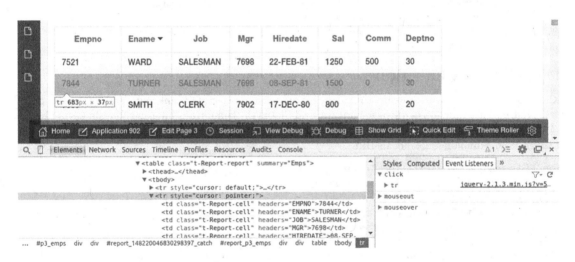

Figure 16-2. *New listeners present on each table row*

Later versions of APEX may show more event listeners for that DOM element.

Method B—React, Respond

The first method works, but requires heavy post-processing. Each time the region refreshes, each row needs processing to reapply the multiple click listeners.

jQuery provides a way to react to a click on a region, identify a specific component clicked, and resolve the action from there.

Prerequisites

The destination URL still needs to be defined for each row, so the method used in the previous example will suffice.

Disable the dynamic action that applies the enable_row_link function. This method will replace that function.

Add Listener to Region

Replace the call to enable_row_link() in the after refresh function with Listing 16-4. The on() function will listen for clicks within the #p4_emps region and act only when a table row is clicked, as per the second parameter. Using this parameter can be compared to defining a dynamic action on the region with an Event Scope of Dynamic.

Listing 16-4. Listen for Click within Row

```
$('#p4_emps').on('click', 'tr', function(event) {
  l_target = $(event.target).closest('tr').find('a.rowlink').attr('href');
  if (l_target)
    window.location=l_target;
});
```

The callback function determines the URL by locating the closest TR based on whatever is clicked, and then finding the URL defined in the anchor element with the rowlink class in that row. The function will only change the window location if a URL was determined, thereby ignoring events on header rows, row totals, and pagination.

Summary

I demonstrated two solutions in this chapter with the same outcome, but the method used in each one was quite different. This highlights yet again how a working solution to a problem may not be the best one.

Choosing a suboptimal solution may impact performance on the page and/or scalability of your application.

Elegance is often an attribute of efficiency, so if your jQuery is verbose and has many moving parts, you may need to reconsider refactoring the code.

Ultimately, this chapter shows how functional APEX applications can be upgraded with minimal effort to make them suitable for a touchscreen-based environment.

CHAPTER 17

■ ■ ■

Customizing Pagination

Search results in reports often span multiple pages. The APEX pagination options are too small for touch devices, let alone some users of desktop machines.

In this chapter, the reader will learn how to upgrade the pagination in a classic report to behave similarly to Google-style search engine pagination. The technique offered might also spur other ideas regarding what can be done with jQuery.

About Pagination

Sets of data rarely fit on one page, which is why building a search page is a common task in APEX development. APEX offers a variety of options for those records that do not fit on the first page of results.

Interactive reports offer basic next/previous links, but further customization requires more work. Classic reports, however, offer the variety shown in Figure 17-1.

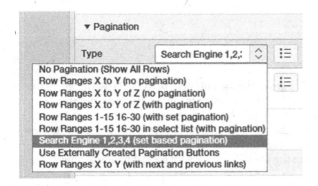

Figure 17-1. *APEX pagination options*

Figure 17-2 shows the default pagination mechanism used in Theme 25, with row ranges in a select list. The UI features are fine for desktop use, but a large list of options in a select list next to short buttons is not suitable for touchscreens.

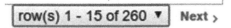

Figure 17-2. *Row ranges in select list*

The example in this chapter will use the search- engine-set-based pagination, which shows multiple pages of results as links with sequential number labeling. The output shown in Figure 17-3 is from a Theme 25 classic report and it would be difficult for users to use effectively on a touchscreen.

1 2 3 4 5 6 7 8 9 10   **Next Set ›**

Figure 17-3. *Theme 25 search engine style, pre-modification*

The example in this chapter will turn those HTML anchors into large buttons suitable for touch interfaces. I'll use Theme 25 since the UI is particularly bad. The templates have improved in the Universal Theme, as shown in Figure 17-4, where it may only require some CSS to add extra padding around the links.

| 1 | 2 | 3 | 4 | 5 | 6 | 7 | 8 | 9 | 10 | Next Set ► |

Figure 17-4. *Theme 42 search engine style*

Note that any style showing a known number of pages or the total number of rows (Z) will lengthen the time required to render the page. This is because in addition to the actual result set, the exact number of rows needs to be determined as to render the pagination set, which can be expensive.

For simple, orderable datasets where the total number of rows is less than 1000, pagination can be more effective than scrolling a large page of results. Reports where fast results using selective criteria wins over sifting through pages of results may be better suited to use the Ranges X-Y with no pagination setting.

Prepare Report

The sample employee table does not have enough rows for this demonstration, so instead create a new report page using Listing 17-1. This SQL will return all the days in the current year that are not the weekend, providing at least 250 rows.

Listing 17-1. Generate Many Rows of Data

```
with this_year as
(select rownum rn, (trunc(sysdate,'yy')+rownum) dt
 from dual
 connect by level < 365
)
select rownum, dt, to_char(dt, 'fmDay')
from this_year
where to_char(dt,'DY') not in ('SAT','SUN')
```

Ensure the report type is classic and add a Static ID of "paginated." Now modify the region attributes to set pagination type to *Search Engine 1,2,3,4*.

You may be interested to note you can also inflate the number of rows returned in an existing report by temporarily adding the following cross join to existing SQL:

```
select * from emp -- existing SQL
cross join (select null from dual connect by level <= 3)
```

The cross join is ANSI syntax that creates a Cartesian product of the two tables, so a query on EMP joined with 3 rows from dual returns 42 rows. The keywords "cross join" could be replaced with a comma. The "connect by" syntax produces the number of rows specified in the final expression, an effective way to conjure data.

Upgrading Pagination

jQuery can be added to the page to convert the simple HTML anchors to larger buttons, with further button styling added in a later step.

Add JavaScript Function

This function converts the basic links to buttons, using jQuery to identify the relevant components of the pagination cells in the designated report. Add Listing 17-2 to the page Function and Global Variable Declaration attribute.

As with other features, the class names and HTML structure have changed slightly between Themes 25 and 42. Uncomment the second variable definition to override the first if you're using Theme 42.

Listing 17-2. Convert Links to Buttons

```
function apply_pagination(report_id) {
  // Note: selector differences across themes
  var selector = ' td.pagination span.fielddata';    // Theme 25
  // var selector = ' span.t-Report-paginationText';  // Theme 42

    // hide single number if one page of results shown
  if ($(report_id+selector+' a').size() == 0)
    $(report_id+selector).css('display','none');
```

```
// transform each link found into a button, converting href to onclick
$(report_id+selector+' a').each(function(){
  $(this).replaceWith('<button class="uButton" onclick="'+$(this).attr('href')+'"
  type="button"><span>'+$(this).text()+'</span></button>');
});

// Theme 25: Next/Prev when over ten pages identified separately, hence can be treated
independently
$(report_id+' td a.uPaginationNext').text('(Next)');
$(report_id+' td a.uPaginationPrev').text('(Prev)');
// Hide in t42, though could differentiate with class suffix --next
// or instead ask user to refine search so next() not needed
$(report_id+' a.t-Report-paginationLink').hide();

}
```

If no more than one page of results is displayed, then the function will remove the pagination area. Otherwise, the jQuery selector locates all pagination anchors and uses `.replaceWith()` replace with the button alternative. Each anchor is processed where `$(this)` can be referenced to harvest the href attribute, which is in turn inserted as the button's onclick event.

The next and previous buttons that are shown when the results are over ten pages are classed differently; hence, they can be handled separately. Harmonizing with the concept that the user may not sift past the first few pages and adjust their criteria instead, you may choose to hide the options instead of re-styling them.

Invoke Function

Convert the links to buttons by invoking the function on page load every time the report is refreshed, which is normally done by navigating to a different page of results.

Without re-invoking the function on the apexafterrerfesh event on the report, the pagination area links will remain displayed in the original format after the report is re-refreshed.

Listing 17-3 needs to be invoked on page load so can be done so using a dynamic action or using the Execute when Page Loads attribute. Once applied, the output will look like Figure 17-5.

Listing 17-3. Convert Links to Buttons

```
// on page load
apply_pagination('#paginated');
// and each time the report is refreshed, typically via pagination
$('#paginated').on('apexafterrefresh', function(e) {
  // reapply conversion of links to buttons
  apply_pagination('#paginated');
});
```

Figure 17-5. Converted buttons, before styling

The list of pages in the report output have now been converted, but still require some extra styling to ensure appropriate spacing around the digits and between the buttons.

Add CSS to Style Buttons

Values may vary depending on your theme, audience, and device. Use Listing 17-4 for your page's inline CSS, which covers Themes 25 and 42. The end result targets usage on touch devices.

Listing 17-4. CSS Styling for Pagination Buttons

```css
/* some room below the report */
td.pagination {
  padding-top: 10px;
}
/* elbow room between buttons */
td.pagination button.uButton {
  margin:0 4px;
  padding: 0px;
}
/* make buttons bigger for tablet fingers */
td.pagination button.uButton span {
  font-size: 150%;
  padding: 10px 15px;
}
/* the 'current' page */
td.pagination b {
  padding: 20px;
  font-size: 200%;
}
/* When larger data sets - next/prev links */
td.pagination a.uPaginationNext
,td.pagination a.uPaginationPrev
,td.pagination t-Report-paginationLink /* Theme 42 */
{
  font-size: 200%;
}
```

The final result is shown in Figure 17-6. This design should make it easy for large fingers to distinguish between links and clearly choose the desired button.

Figure 17-6. *Updated pagination options*

Tweak the numbers specified within the CSS to set sizes and padding to a desired level. Remember, this is easiest done first by inspecting browser elements and modifying values in the browser directly. Then copy your desired values into the embedded CSS.

Alternatively, you could use a more contemporary style, inspired by what's available in the Universal Theme.

Summary

The pagination widget is one of many areas in your applications that could be upgraded in some form to cater for your intended device and/or audience.

Customizations in APEX come in many forms. In this case, instead of attempting to modify the report template, jQuery can be added to respond to and convert outputs from their original form.

PART V

Diversifying Techniques

CHAPTER 18

■ ■ ■

Customizing Item Help

A simple but frequent request is for the ability to customize the help displayed when clicking on APEX item labels. By default, this help comes from data set at design time by the developer. However, it's possible to allow users to maintain this data and display help source from custom content by combining jQuery with database processes.

Define Help Data

A few options exist in regard to where to store help information for items. Each option has advantages and disadvantages, so you need to decide what balance suits your project the best.

Design Time

The Help Text attribute for page items shown in Figure 18-1 is ideal for item help text as this is the source used when the user clicks on the help icon for the relevant item, as shown in Figure 18-2.

Figure 18-1. *Item help text in the page designer*

Figure 18-2. *Item help text shown at runtime*

The main disadvantage of this location is the text is required at design time as there is no published API to modify the content. Fickle users may also require updates to this text and this means a change by the developer to the application.

In the Universal Theme, the help icon will only appear for items with help defined. In prior themes, this link was the item label itself, and we'll do the same in this example since all relevant fields will have a label. However, we still need a place to store the column help where the user can maintain it.

UI Defaults

User Interface Defaults (UI Defaults) are attributes the developer can use to define the standard look and feel for columns in the database prior to building an application. These attribute selections are carried through as forms and reports are built, including item help.

APIs are available to update these defaults and, therefore, could be used as a location for storing updatable help content. Pages could be built around maintaining help text and be exposed to end users, but this would only impact pages yet to be built. Modifying UI Defaults will not affect existing pages, so this process would need to be completed before building the application.

UI Defaults can be created through the SQL Workshop Utilities module. Once defined for a table, an API call could be used to update the help text:

```
begin
APEX_UI_DEFAULT_UPDATE.UPD_ITEM_HELP (
    p_table_name          => 'EMP'
    ,p_column_name        => 'ENAME'
    ,p_help_text          => 'Enter the employee name');
end;
/
```

The help text could then be queried using the APEX dictionary view APEX_UI_DEFAULTS_COLUMNS.

Custom Tables

Utilizing your own set of tables to store item help data is always a viable solution. Custom tables allow the flexibility to define help at page level or a more generic column name level.

The custom table would need to record application and page number, which allows re-use across applications. The item name in the data format P1_ITEM would be used as cross-reference when the user clicks on the help link and, of course, a column for storing the help content:

```
create table item_help
 (app_id     number not null
 ,page_id    number not null
 ,item_name  varchar2(30) not null
 ,help_text  varchar2(400) not null
 ,constraint item_help_pk
    PRIMARY KEY (app_id, page_id, item_name)
);
```

There is no clear disadvantage to using this solution, but since every reader will have a different set of application and page IDs, I will defer to the final option for the demonstration.

Depending on your application, there may be replication of help where the same logical item appears across multiple pages, but a well-designed maintenance application can help mitigate that.

Column Comments

While not strictly meta-data, Oracle technologists favor database column comments as a semi-permanent documentation location for database columns.

The comments could be worded with the end user in mind; however, updates to these comments are done using data definition language (DDL), not with an SQL update. This may deter some DBAs when defining boundaries of a help maintenance application.

Database column comments will be used as the help source for the demonstration in this chapter. Listing 18-1 will apply help for many of the columns in the emp table.

Listing 18-1. Add Column Help for the Emp Table

```
comment on column emp.ename is 'Enter the employee name';
comment on column emp.job is 'What does the employee do?';
comment on column emp.mgr is 'Who is the employee''s manager?';
comment on column emp.hiredate is 'When was this person hired?';
comment on column emp.sal is 'What is this person''s monthly salary?';
comment on column emp.comm is 'How much commission do they receive?';
```

Comments defined like this can be queried from dictionary view USER_COL_COMMENTS. One disadvantage of this method, however, is there may be additional fields on the page that don't map to a database column, which can also be true for UI Defaults.

Querying dictionary tables can also slow the user experience, but this can be mitigated with materialized views.

Identifying the Table Name

All solutions also have the issue of identifying the table relevant to the item, except the custom table definition used, as described earlier.

A potential workaround might be to add the table name in the comments attribute of each item. Another idea would be to populate a JavaScript variable on page load, which presumes all columns on the page belong to a particular table, but it will suffice for this example.

Add the following to the Execute When Page Loads page attribute for the EMP form:

```
f_table_name = 'EMP';
```

Modify Label Template

It is not necessary to modify the label template in the APEX 5.0 Universe Theme 42 since no help icon is displayed if no text is entered in the Item Help attribute. This example will use the item label to invoke help.

In earlier versions of APEX, the default help functionality needs to be disabled. One method of doing so is to edit the label template and replace the call to the pop-up help function with the following:

```
javascript:void(0);
```

The customized event listener will replace this functionality.

Replace Default Help with Event Listener

The major jQuery component in this example is the event listener for the item label attribute. This will need to respond to a click on the item label and show a pop up with the relevant help text.

The pop up could be an inline dialog with a simple report on where the help sourced, but that would limit the fun in a book about jQuery.

Instead, it will behave similarly to the way the Theme 25 templates displayed help. The jQuery will call a PL/SQL process to source the help text, and then a dialog will be rendered around on the content.

The function used to display the help would be useful across the application so it shouldn't be included in the page attributes. Instead, such JavaScript should reside in JavaScript files included in the application via the User Interface Details in Shared Components.

This requirement is the perfect time to demonstrate how to store and refer to JavaScript files in your application. This modularization process should be done with all your JavaScript and CSS, just like you would move anonymous PL/SQL blocks to stored packages.

Load Static File

Listing 18-2 defines the function that sends the item and table name to a PL/SQL process in order to locate the relevant help text. The label parameter will be used as the dialog title, invoked much the same way as Theme 25 templates display help.

Listing 18-2. Item Help JavaScript Function

```
// display help text for a given item
function item_help(p_item, p_table, p_label) {
  apex.debug('p_item:'+p_item);
  apex.debug('p_table:'+p_table);
  apex.server.process
    ("CB_ITEM_HELP"
    ,{ // pData
       x01 : p_item
      ,x02 : p_table
     }
    ,{ // pOptions
       dataType:"text"
      ,loadingIndicator : "#"+p_item+"_LABEL"
     }
  ).done(function(pData) {
    // invoke dialog with data PL/SQL returns
    d=$('<div id="apex_popup_help_area" style="margin:15px">'+pData+'</div>');
    d.dialog({title:p_label,width:500,height:350,show:"drop",hide:"drop"})
  });
}
```

The function sends the table and item name to the PL/SQL procedure that returns the help text. A loading indicator will be shown next to the label while waiting for the database to respond. The defer function executes upon completion of the PL/SQL. A DOM string is constructed surrounding the text, and then it gets rendered as a jQuery dialog.

Use the relevant source file associated with this book, or save the source in an appropriately named JavaScript file, such as item_help.js.

Load the file as a Static Application File in Shared Components, as shown in Figure 18-3.

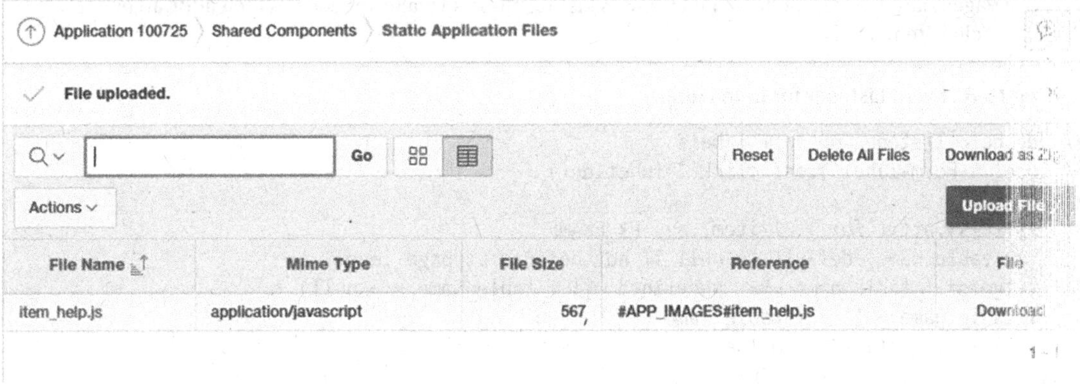

File Name ↑	Mime Type	File Size	Reference	File
item_help.js	application/javascript	567	#APP_IMAGES#item_help.js	Download

Figure 18-3. *JavaScript loaded as static file*

The reference provided can then be inserted as a JavaScript URL in the User Interface Details of the desktop theme, as shown in Figure 18-4.

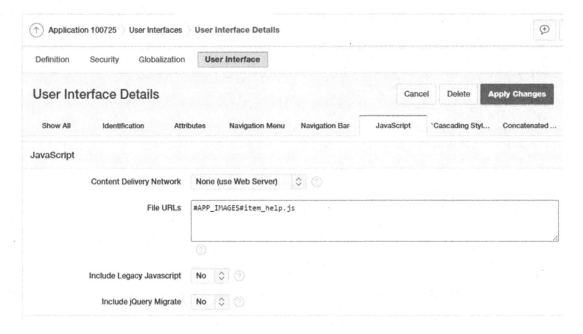

Figure 18-4. *File included in desktop user interface*

This file will now be included in all pages of the application. Hence, the function will also be available for reference in all pages.

Add Listener to Global Page

Now all that remains for the help listener is to invoke the item help whenever any item labels are clicked. Create a Page Load dynamic action that executes Listing 18-3 as JavaScript code, which adds an event listener to click item labels.

Listing 18-3. Event Listener for Item Label

```
// add help listener on form labels
$('label.t-Form-label').on('click', function() {
  item_help
    ($(this).attr('for') // item, eg: P3_ENAME
    // table name, default to null if not defined at page level
    ,(typeof f_table_name === 'undefined' || f_table_name === null) ?
    f_table_name = '' : f_table_name
    ,$(this).text() // item label
  );
});
```

It's worth noting the class selector may be `.uHelpLink`, `.uRequired`, or `.uOptional`, depending on the application theme and item template used.

The item_help() function's actual parameter values come from information about the clicked label. The second parameter looks the most complicated, but it's like an NVL2 expression. If the f_table_name hasn't been defined or is null, then an empty string is passed. Otherwise, use the variable's value. And you may think Oracle doesn't handle nulls well?

The first parameter extracts the item name from the for attribute in the label, as highlighted in Figure 18-5.

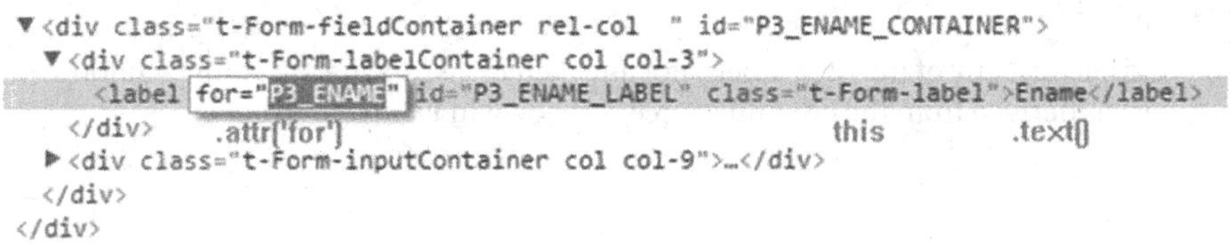

Figure 18-5. *Using DOM attribute to mine data*

The third parameter uses the clicked label text. This becomes the dialog title.

The labels will now respond to clicks, but the PL/SQL callback it invokes needs to be defined.

Define PL/SQL Process

The PL/SQL callback is invoked by the JavaScript to return the help text for the item label clicked. Since this process would be applicable application-wide, define an Application Process via Shared Components and set the processing point to On Demand.

Call the process CB_ITEM_HELP and use Listing 18-4 as the source.

Listing 18-4. PL/SQL Callback for Item Help

```
-- Fetch item help
declare
  l_item   varchar2(30) := apex_application.g_x01;
  l_table  varchar2(30) := apex_application.g_x02;
  l_help   varchar2(512);
begin
  -- Fetch item help for provided table/column
  apex_debug.message('CB_ITEM_HELP => '||l_table||':'||l_item);
  select coalesce(comments, 'No help for this item.')
  into l_help
  from user_col_comments
  where (table_name, column_name)
    = (
    select l_table, item_source
    from apex_application_page_items
    where application_id = :APP_ID
    and item_name = l_item);

  htp.prn(l_help);
exception
  when no_data_found then
    htp.prn('Column not found.');
end fetch_help;
```

Secondary to identifying the relevant table, the relevant column can be derived from the item source in form—, for example translating the P3_ENAME item to the database source column needed to fetch the comment. Since this example uses database columns to define help text, this harmonizes nicely with using item source, but it would not be suitable for extra non-database items.

Runtime Test

Run the EMP form page and click on any of the item labels, not any help icons. A jQuery pop-up window will slide in and display help text as derived from the column source, as shown in Figure 18-6.

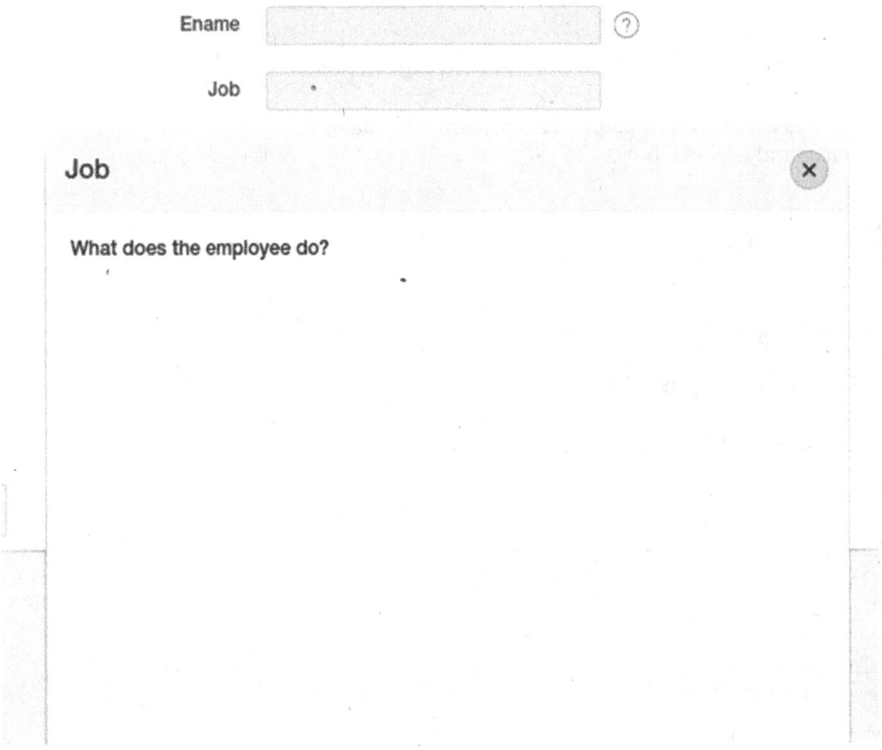

Figure 18-6. Customized help output

Clicking on the DEPTNO column will state no help exists, not no data found. If another field were added, no rows would be returned as the column would not map to a database field.

Performance

Performance is often on my mind, and there are few considerations to be made this this example. Sometimes it's also about giving the user immediate feedback instead of waiting for the AJAX call to return. There are a few considerations in this example.

Modifying Workflow

As previously mentioned, the pop up could be defined as an inline dialog on the global page and within it a report could be formatted to show the help text. This means the pop up could be shown immediately and a spinner shown while the report refreshes. The user is therefore given instant feedback that something is happening.

Modify Spinner

A more prominent spinner could be shown, as explored in Chapter 9. Listing 18-5 modifies the item_help function, removing the loadingIndicator and replacing it with the showSpinner() function. It returns an object so it can be removed in the deferred function.

Listing 18-5. Item Help Update

```
// display help text for a given item
function item_help(p_item, p_table, p_label) {
  apex.debug('p_item:'+p_item);
  apex.debug('p_table:'+p_table);
  $loading = apex.util.showSpinner('body');
  apex.server.process
    ("CB_ITEM_HELP"
    ,{ // pData
       x01 : p_item
      ,x02 : p_table
     }
    ,{ // pOptions
       dataType:"text"
     }
  ).done(function(pData) {
    // invoke dialog with data PL/SQL returns
    $loading.remove();
    d=apex.jQuery('<div id="apex_popup_help_area" style="margin:15px">'+pData+'</div>');
    d.dialog({title:p_label,width:500,height:350,show:"drop",hide:"drop"})
  });
}
```

The need from showing a spinner can be mitigated if the information was available locally.

Caching Information

In a highly tuned Oracle Forms application, reference codes fetched from the database would be stored in local data structures to hasten response when needed next time. This was often done using arrays indexed by a variable character string.

The same can be done in JavaScript. Once help is fetched for an item, the help text could be stored in an array. Indexed by the item name, it would be possible to retrieve if the user repeatedly opened help items prior to submitting the page or moving on:

```
var arr = []; // array definition

arr[p_item] = pData; // assign result to element indexed by item
```

Then you can use that value if the index exists instead of invoking an AJAX call to fetch item help. Alternatively, the JavaScript code could be generated from PL/SQL as part of the page render, so even the first fetch for help is fast.

Touch Lag

The requirement of instant response is more pronounced in touch devices so you can indicate to the users that their tap was effective. Due to the input method of touch devices, a small 300ms delay is experienced on the touchscreen as it waits to determine if it was a tap or a drag.

Small libraries such as TouchPunch.js allow definition of events that ignore the delay, a useful feature in APEX applications to reduce unnecessary lag. Including the Touch Punch JavaScript file on your page allows immediate interaction through custom events such as touchstart, removing the 300ms delay as the device waits to see if it was a touch or drag/hold.

Summary

Once again many options exist for defining a custom solution for a common problem. In this case, the jQuery component is independent to the source of the data, which makes the solution more versatile.

The amount of code in this chapter was minimal, but it repeats a common pattern of JavaScript that invokes some PL/SQL that returns fresh data from the database ready for the browser to act upon.

■ ■ ■

File Browse Validation

Browsers offer native functionality for selecting files to upload. APEX then provides the smarts to convert the incoming data into a BLOB ready for database storage with the File Browse item component.

A common request is to validate the file before the page is submitted—for instance, limiting uploadable file size. Doing so can prevent excess network traffic if the page is prevented from loading the file until it meets size and type requirements. There is no point validating something in the database when it can be done on the web page.

This chapter not only applies this practical example, but it helps you locate the information you might have needed to solve the problem yourself. As my high school teachers always requested, I will "show my work," with the aim to help you practice for the jQuery feature requests you may encounter in the future.

Using Google to Find the Answer

Internet search engines are an amazing tool, regardless of your profession, but the trick to using them effectively is in knowing what the question is. To start with, let's determine how to restrict the file browse input to only images.

When looking for code snippets, knowing a related function name such as Oracle's INSTR can help you isolate results. However, in an unfamiliar language, it can be difficult to know what to search for and where best to find results.

In this section, I share my thought processes when exploring the web for a solution.

Gathering Information

Before searching the vast Web, you should determine what information you have available. This process can help isolate potential keywords or, at the very least, give forum volunteers the opportunity to know as much about your problem beyond what you can describe. You may even stumble upon enough information to solve the problem on the spot.

Gathering information starts by building a basic test case, which can help later on if using the forums. Build a new blank page in your application and then add a static region. Add a button to this region to submit the page and an item using the File Browse type.

Since it would be desirable to have this feature work on selection of a file, create a dynamic action on the file browser item that executes JavaScript on change. Before attempting to solve the problem, output relevant information available using the attributes described in the code help shown in Chapter 5:

```
console.log($(this.triggeringElement).val()); // item value
console.log(this.triggeringElement);          // DOM element
console.log(this.browserEvent);               // event details
```

Figure 19-1 shows the output once the selection of a file has been made. The value simply results the filename, which may be useful for file type validation. The fakepath prefix is due to the browser complying with security principles.

Figure 19-1. *Console log output after file selection*

The triggeringElement syntax returns the DOM object for the input item, which has been useful in previous examples used in this book.

I've expanded the event object to show note the target attribute. Not only is the P19_FILE input item named, making it an obvious point of interest, experience tells me most of the required information for an event can be found in that node.

When editing an APEX component like an item or region, then change the type, different attributes are offered. You will find the same in browser events, and some of these attributes match back to declarative settings within APEX.

Scanning through the attributes I found jackpot, shown in Figure 19-2. I drilled further to find the exact information I would need to validate file selection, all accessible with JavaScript.

Figure 19-2. Drill down into browserEvent attributes

With this information you may not even need to hit the Web, though you may still need help bringing this together in a solution for APEX. You may also wish to find out why files are represented as an array and if this is something to consider.

Using Google

When I use Google, I expect the answer to be found within the first set of results, given the right criteria. There are certain sites I've learned to look out for and others to ignore.

The pattern I use for searches typically involves three components, which is why it's important to think about what your question actually is:

1. Technology

2. Component

3. Action

For example, when searching for a way to restrict the file input to images, I might combine variations of the following:

1. jQuery, or Oracle APEX, or both

2. file browse

3. validate file type, or

Without enough specificity, you can find yourself weeding out too much chaff. The day I wrote this section, I found myself searching for a regular expression to return first element in a delimited string. I tried variations of "regexp delimited string first word," but it wasn't until I added "oracle" did I find my answer in the first result by a trusted forum contributor.

Since I'm not as familiar with jQuery as I am with PL/SQL, a concise search prefixed with jQuery will suffice. To return the selected option within a select list, "jquery selected option" returns the effective-looking results in Figure 19-3.

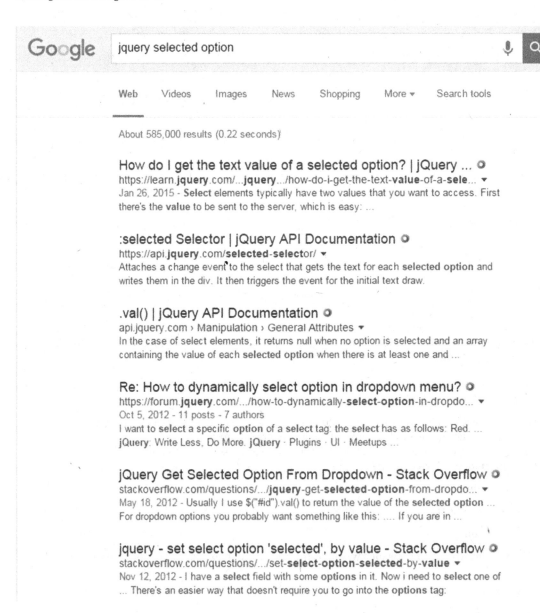

Figure 19-3. *Google results for a common jQuery snippet*

When searching for code snippets, I find Google does a good job at providing a variety of sites, which also tends to improve the chance of finding exactly what you need. Documentation sites are always a good source that may provide a simple description of the feature with a concise example.

I also find stackoverflow a reliable source as good answers bubble to the top fairly well—more on this in the next section.

Exploring Viable Results

With the variation of searches, I came across a number of viable solutions that could be adopted for APEX, some more ready to go than others. This selection of results came from different searches so I'll highlight the notable part of the page and provide the URL so you can see it all in context if you wish.

Ultimately, I find it once again demonstrates the diversity of solutions available. (Occasionally, you'll come across something so elegant and concise you may weep a little.) Whichever the choice, we can all still learn from the discarded results.

How to Have jQuery Restrict File Types on Upload

Like many stackoverflow results for jQuery, this result can be applied regardless of backend. APEX item #P19_FILE can be substituted in as #my_file_field so the snippet could be tested straight away. You could also systematically remove each chained function to reverse engineer the solution, as shown in Figure 19-4.

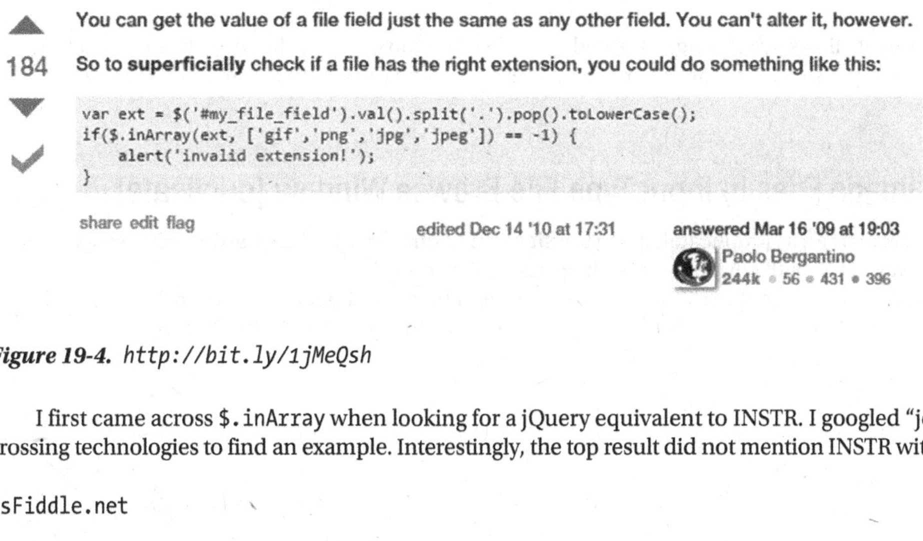

You can get the value of a file field just the same as any other field. You can't alter it, however.

184   So to **superficially** check if a file has the right extension, you could do something like this:

```
var ext = $('#my_file_field').val().split('.').pop().toLowerCase();
if($.inArray(ext, ['gif','png','jpg','jpeg']) == -1) {
    alert('invalid extension!');
}
```

share edit flag   edited Dec 14 '10 at 17:31   answered Mar 16 '09 at 19:03

Paolo Bergantino
244k ● 56 ● 431 ● 396

Figure 19-4. `http://bit.ly/1jMeQsh`

I first came across `$.inArray` when looking for a jQuery equivalent to INSTR. I googled "jquery instr," crossing technologies to find an example. Interestingly, the top result did not mention INSTR within the page:

jsFiddle.net

Sites like jsFiddle allow a great platform to test solutions involving JavaScript, which makes it a great tool for forums when demonstrating problems. Figure 19-5 shows how the fiddle creator defined a solution that defines basic HTML and CSS, and then supplies a JavaScript snippet that could be pasted directly in APEX page attribute with an adjustment to the #image reference to #P19_FILE.

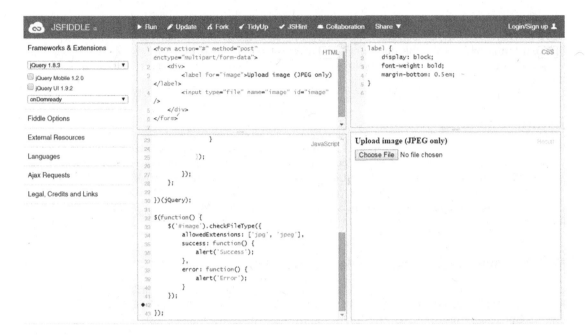

Figure 19-5. `http://bit.ly/1jMgDgW`

The bottom right allows live testing of the code and this solution proves to be ready to go, bar defining exactly what happens on success or failure. In this case, it you would probably clear the P19_FILE item selection.

Show Only Image Files In Input Type File Browse Window [duplicate]

When a question is marked as [duplicate], it's a sure sign you're onto a common question with a good answer not far away, often with commentary to help assess the code.

Figure 19-6 shows an accept attribute for the input item that could be injected from APEX using the Custom Attributes item setting. This feature is particularly nifty as it also limits the files listed in the dialog.

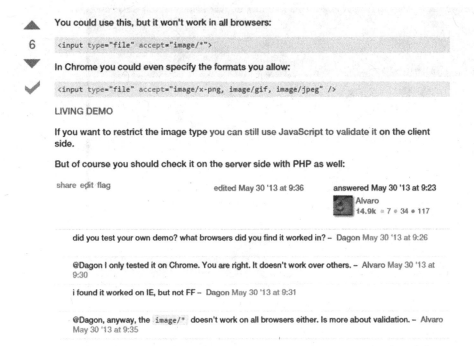

You could use this, but it won't work in all browsers:

```
<input type="file" accept="image/*">
```

In Chrome you could even specify the formats you allow:

```
<input type="file" accept="image/x-png, image/gif, image/jpeg" />
```

LIVING DEMO

If you want to restrict the image type you can still use JavaScript to validate it on the client side.

But of course you should check it on the server side with PHP as well:

share edit flag   edited May 30 '13 at 9:36   answered May 30 '13 at 9:23
                                                                     Alvaro
                                                                     14.9k ● 7 ● 34 ● 117

did you test your own demo? what browsers did you find it worked in? – Dagon May 30 '13 at 9:26

@Dagon I only tested it on Chrome. You are right. It doesn't work over others. – Alvaro May 30 '13 at 9:30

i found it worked on IE, but not FF – Dagon May 30 '13 at 9:31

@Dagon, anyway, the `image/*` doesn't work on all browsers either. Is more about validation. – Alvaro May 30 '13 at 9:35

Figure 19-6. *http://bit.ly/1Z6YScx (sans code)*

Pay particular attention to the commentary by the author and contributors. You may find different results depending on the browser being used. This is common for attributes newer to the HTML specification, and Figure 19-7 shows how the site `caniuse.com` can provide details on compliance.

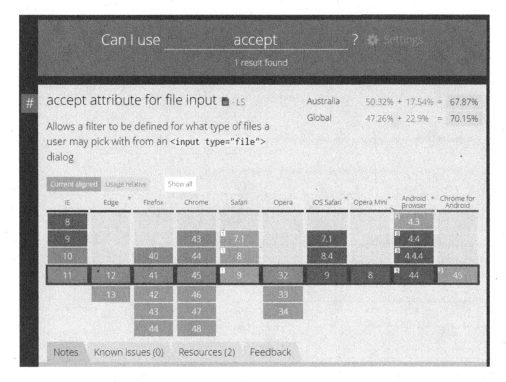

Figure 19-7. *http://caniuse.com/#search=accept*

The author provides a link to solve the problem using JavaScript instead on the client side, but rightly recommends validation on the server side as well. This should apply for any data being validated; there are a variety of ways to circumnavigate any client validation.

Using Forums

Search results often provide links to questions already asked in forums, but feel free to ask your own if you're struggling to translate the examples to your own work or the examples are too old. Communities of volunteers are waiting to give you assistance.

It is also important to know and describe what you are trying to solve. In the case of validating file type it's fairly clear, but the goal can be forgotten and you only describe what has been attempted.

This is known as the *xy problem*, described succinctly at http://xyproblem.info/, where attempting to do *x* you ask for help with *y*, which may have nothing to do with *x*.

In addition to asking a question, you should also be prepared to provide a basic test case, which can be vital in obtaining a speedy answer.

Stack Overflow

I find this particular forum useful for jQuery, JavaScript, CSS, and generally all things Web. New users are given education on forum use and incrementally given more power to interact with the site, as your experience grows and skills proven.

The forum format established at stackoverflow is popular because it works well, saving future readers from sifting through old, irrelevant discussions. Any reader of AskTom.oracle.com may have experienced this.

The example in Figure 19-6 shows an answer accepted by the original poster as signified by the green tick. Other contributors have "up" or "down" voted the response, allowing better answers to bubble to the top of the list.

Be aware the answer with the most votes might not be the best or most current. Pay attention to the comments on each response, which can also be "up" voted for relevance.

Test cases in stackoverflow are best provided as a jsFiddle, but at the very least provide relevant content from the DOM and what has been attempted.

OTN Forums

All APEX-related questions are best asked on the OTN forum. Some jQuery-related questions are also addressed here, particularly when tightly coupled with the APEX product.

The forum infrastructure isn't as sophisticated, but comes with the same basic premise. Ask good questions, provide test cases where possible, and remember to provide details such as APEX version as this will influence the answer.

Don't be afraid to ask questions. You should find a positive feedback loop with your skill level increasing as you become known in the forums.

Translating to APEX

The prospective solutions can be tested in APEX, but they are all applied slightly differently.

Validate File Extension Using File String

The example from Figure 19-4 has the smallest snippet that could be added for use in the dynamic action. Listing 19-1 shows a slightly modified version that will also clear the selection if invalid.

Listing 19-1. ValidateFile Extension Using File String

```
// determine single file extension
var ext = $('#P19_FILE').val().split('.').pop().toLowerCase();

if($.inArray(ext, ['gif','png','jpg','jpeg']) == -1) {
  $('#P19_FILE').val(''); // clear selection
  alert('invalid extension ('+ext+')');
}
```

Validate File Extension Using Input Attribute

The accept attribute can be added to the Custom Attributes field in the P19_FILE file browse item, as shown in Figure 19-8.

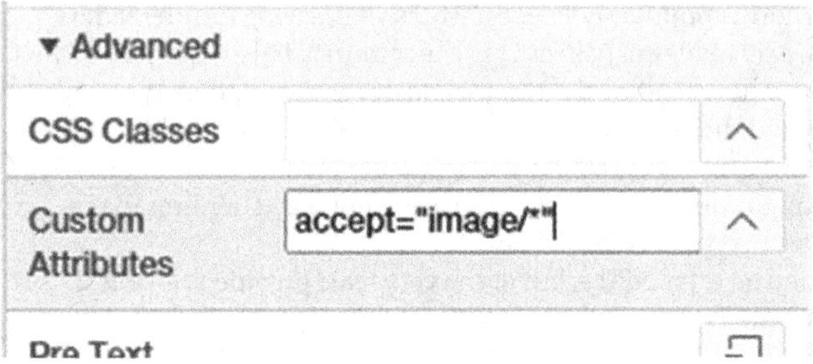

Figure 19-8. *File browse custom attributes*

This solution would need to be tested on browsers your application may run on.

Validating File Size

None of the search results mentioned size, though Figure 19-2 showed it was available for use. Listing 19-2 shows JavaScript that could also be applied in the on change dynamic action to ensure file sizes are kept under one million bytes (approximately 1mb).

Listing 19-2. Validate File Size

```
// validate single file size
var size = this.browserEvent.target.files[0].size;

if (size > 1000000) {
  $('#P19_FILE').val(''); // clear selection
  alert('too large ('+size+')');
}
```

This solution is presuming only one file can be selected, since only the first element in the array of files is checked.

Multiple Files

File input items can be modified to accept multiple selections simply by adding the attribute `multiple` to the same Custom Attributes field modified for the image type.

While the transmission of multiple files would be more complex, calculating the total size of the selected files can be done by iterating the array of files. Up until now, we've only referred to the first (and only) array element.

Listing 19-3 demonstrates a typical JavaScript loop, iterating through all file selections to derive a total size for the file set.

Listing 19-3. Total Multiple File Sizes

```
// add up size of multiple files
var totsize = 0;
for (var i = 0, f; f = this.browserEvent.target.files[i]; i++) {
  totsize = totsize + f.size;
}
console.log(this.browserEvent.target.files.length+' files, total size:'+totsize);
```

The output will include the number of files in addition to the total sum in bytes.

Summary

This chapter was more about learning to fish than accepting the gift of free meat. I offered an insight into the process a developer may go through in deriving a solution from multiple technologies.

When you use these skills, the application is now capable of validating file data at the client, rather than waiting until the page is submitted to validate the data. Client-side validation is a fair consideration and offers advantages to the user and framework, but all data should still be re-validated at the server.

Community is important. I would love to see more developers appear on Oracle forums giving back to the community while improving themselves at the same time. All it takes is a few minutes a day to skim through current posts to find anything that may be relevant, and perhaps even contribute a response. Asking questions even helps the Oracle team assess the types of problems developers typically experience.

■ ■ ■

CSS Media Queries

The ability to discern between devices and hardware capabilities is a growing need as the smart-device market expands from blackberries to mobiles, "phablets," tablets, laptops, desktops, TVs, glasses, watches, and cars. One aspect is responsiveness where you see web pages mold to the size available, but there are other functions where media queries can aid the APEX developer to delivering a better user experience.

Simple yet effective solutions can be applied in APEX just using CSS media queries alone—you'll see some later in the chapter. However, since this book is all about integrating jQuery with APEX, I'll start with how you can use jQuery to make decisions based on the outcome CSS media queries.

What Is a CSS Media Query?

A CSS media query is an expression around standard CSS that can make it conditional based on the type of media and attributes such as size and orientation. For example, the following snippet using the @media syntax applies the CSS it surrounds only when the media expression identifies a computer screen (including smartphones) in portrait orientation:

```
/* When in portrait, hide anything with given class */
@media screen and (orientation:portrait) {
  .landscape_only {
    display:none;
  }
}
```

If the content becomes large and you need to modularize, you can conditionally link style sheets based upon criteria such as media type and orientation, media type and width, and so forth. The following example links a style sheet in cases when a screen-oriented device is used with the screen held in portrait orientation:

```
<link rel="stylesheet" type"text/css"
  media="screen and (orientation:portrait)"
  href="my-portrait.css" />
```

Note all CSS files still download, but only those relevant are applied to the page.

You can see the syntax is not foreign from CSS. The following site provides a clear illustration of what attributes are available and when they return true:

cssmediaqueries.com

The type of media is most accessibility related, and contemporary units are left wanting. For instance, they are unable to differentiate between a computer screen and handheld device. Instead, developers need to rely on comparing dimensions to known devices. Nuances aside, there are some clear, stable options to help improve the user experience.

Identifying Device Type

It is not possible to identify device type directly using CSS media queries. Instead, it is derived by ratio and size boundaries. If you need to target a specific device, the following site is a reference for major device types:

https://css-tricks.com/snippets/css/media-queries-for-standard-devices/

For instance, Figure 20-1 shows the CSS required to identify an Apple watch.

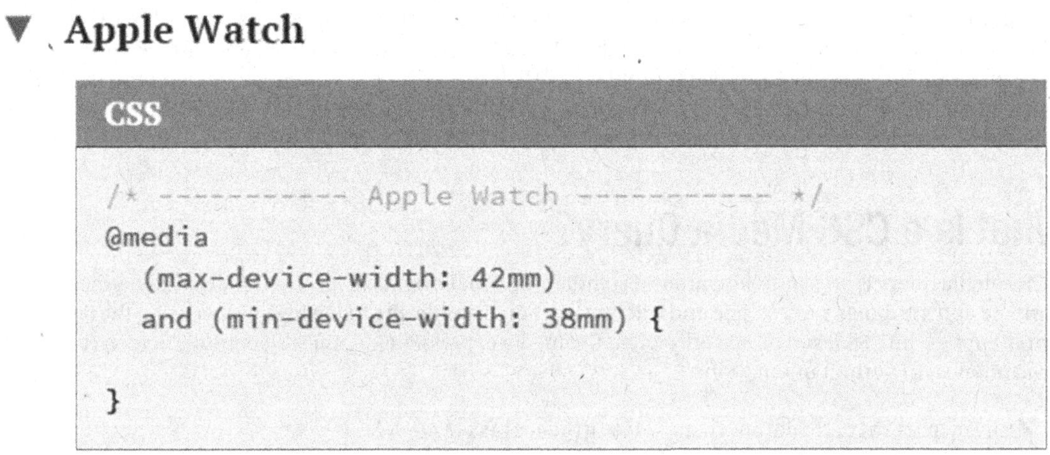

▼ Apple Watch

```
CSS

/* ------------ Apple Watch ------------ */
@media
    (max-device-width: 42mm)
    and (min-device-width: 38mm) {

}
```

Figure 20-1. *css-tricks.com identifies Apple watch with CSS*

In most cases, coding to this granularity can be counterproductive. In reality, device width is typically the only metric used to decide when to toggle style or modify functionality.

Native JavaScript can also determine width, but exact attributes differ between browsers. The following jQuery wrapper handles the complexity:

```
$(window).width()
```

Alternatively, the user agent information can be farmed for details such as operating system and device information. A jQuery library called Modernizr can deconstruct the string to provide a variety of information about the device. A PL/SQL library called Categorizr has similar methods to do the same. Figure 20-2 shows the string value returned from the native navigator.userAgent property.

Figure 20-2. *User agent returned in console*

CSS media queries still make the ideal source of truth for information a typical APEX developer would need, but often what we need is a way to interrogate this information within jQuery logic.

Applying jQuery Logic Based on Media Queries

While creating my submission for the ODTUG APEX Gaming Competition, I needed to execute some jQuery only when the screen width became narrow enough that I needed to rearrange content. I set this boundary at 400 pixels.

It's not possible to use the media query as an expression in jQuery unless you're using libraries like Modernizr as a proxy to this information:

```
Modernizr.mq('(min-width: 400px)')
```

For smaller applications where you don't want to incorporate another library, you can still communicate media query outcomes by modifying a property in the media query for later interrogation by jQuery.

The jQuery width() wrapper seems appropriate. However, height and width browser dimensions do not always match between CSS and JavaScript, where the latter differs between browsers. The particulars are not worth going into detail here, but you should be aware of them since decisions often get made based on browser size.

The following jQuery logic will often apply at a different browser width to the media query method:

```
if ($(window).width() <= 400)
```

The media query will be consistent across browsers:

```
@media screen and (max-width: 400px){
  /* CSS for thin devices here */
}
```

CSS is conditional on the media environment and jQuery returns these attributes, so consistency can be achieved in the measurement by signaling jQuery through CSS properties.

For instance, if a component property is set to LEFT on portrait and RIGHT in landscape, jQuery can interrogate the component to determine the attribute value. This logic can be used to communicate anything that CSS might detect to jQuery using a little ingenuity. The following CSS uses the content property to set whatever value required to control jQuery logic on a component where the attributes have no effect:

```
@media screen and (max-width: 400px){
  #t_Header { float : left;  content : "handheld"; }
}
@media screen and (min-width: 401px){
  #t_Header { float : right; content : "I am > 400px"; }
}
```

The following expression compares the content attribute value based on the media query applied at that moment:

```
if ($('#t_Header').css('content') == 'handheld') {
  // screen max width is 400px, do work for small device

}
```

I would recommend refactoring this expression into a function call so you can test the same condition throughout your application without repeating code:

```
function is_handheld() {
  // usage: if (is_handheld()) {}
  return ($('#t_Header').css('content') == 'handheld');
}
```

Any code that may need to be repeated like this should be turned into some form of method, regardless of language.

Using CSS to Configure Printer Layout

Despite decades dreaming of a paperless office, the ability to send a web page to a printer and have a readable printout is still a must in an enterprise environment, This includes hiding components that don't belong on a piece of paper such as menus, buttons, and images in some cases.

Printer-Friendly Templates

There is a ninth parameter to the APEX page function that is not often mentioned. It requests APEX to display the page in a printer-friendly mode. When applied, the document states that APEX suppresses display tabs and navigation bars, and all items are displayed as text instead of form elements:

f?p=App:Page:Session:Request:Debug:ClearCache:itemNames:itemValues:PrinterFriendly

You will find page templates with a printer-friendly template class in many APEX themes that exclude these components from the template definition. The Universal Theme currently has no such template but does suppress some page elements, but you might like to get specific or target anything left behind.

In addition to the declarative condition type shown in Figure 20-3, you can use a substitution string to determine if the page is in printer-friendly mode.

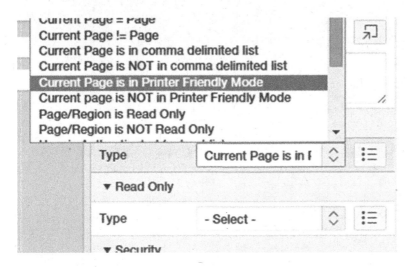

Figure 20-3. *Declarative condition types*

The substitution string can be used like any other, shown here with the PL/SQL syntax:

```
V('PRINTER_FRIENDLY')
```

These features mean you don't need to use a specific page template to remove content from the printer, only adding conditions to components left by the APEX engine. However, this means the page needs to be rendered in printer-friendly mode before invoking the print dialog. CSS media queries can mitigate this need as they will apply as soon as the browser's print preview is opened.

Identifying Components for Exclusion

Before going too much further, it's worth having a look to see what may need to be hidden from the printed output, but without the printer-friendly mode enabled. Figure 20-4 shows the Chrome browser print preview using the Employee report in the Universal Theme application.

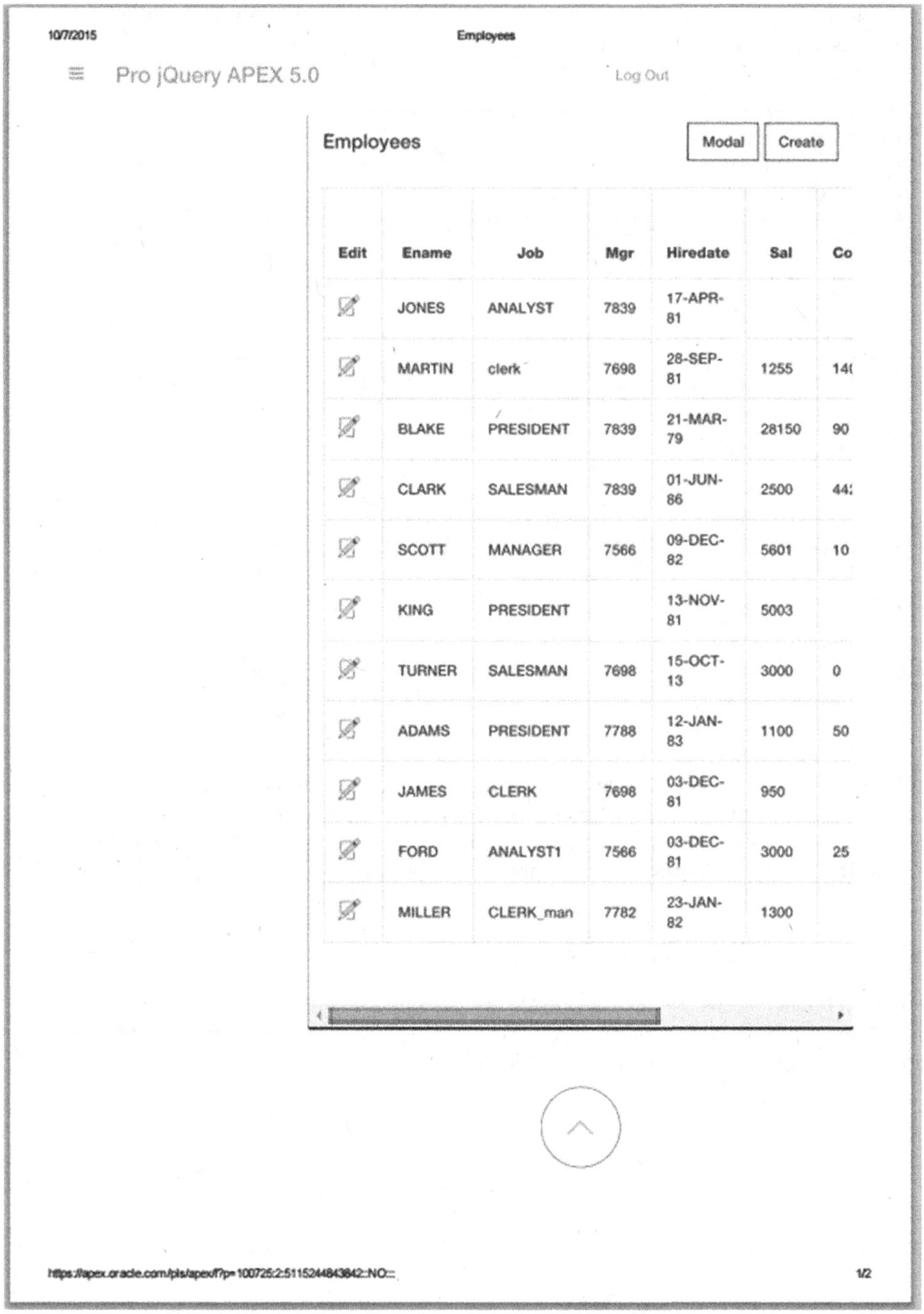

Figure 20-4. Universal Theme print preview, sidebar menu open

The output is not optimized for saving trees since one-third of the page is consumed by the navigation menu. It would be nice to also exclude buttons and in some cases add information that would provide context to the printed document.

Figure 20-5 shows a screenshot where I inspected part of the menu and moved my mouse up, hovering over each parent element until I found the topmost menu tag.

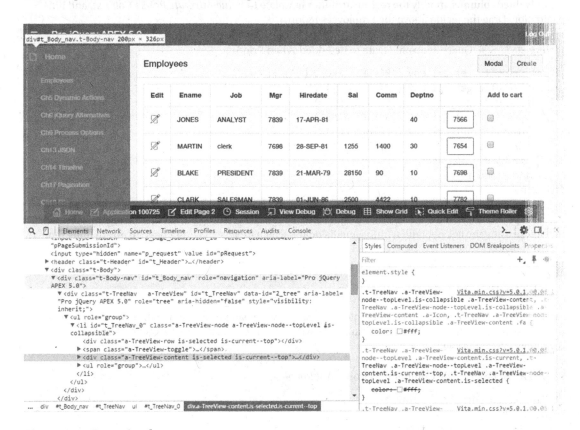

Figure 20-5. *Inspecting the page*

Using this method, I found a collection of IDs and classes that I would like to not include on the printed page:

- #t_Body_nav: This class represents the navigation menu.

- .t-Button: This class identifies buttons I found on the page.

- .t-Body-topButton: This class identifies the faint circular button that sends the user back to the top of the page.

- .t-Header: This class could be used if you also want to remove the header bar across the top.

- .t-Footer: Likewise, the footer text could also be hidden.

And since I used the Inspect Element tool and applied display:none to the page straight away to check the output, I also found the body content margin needs to be restored after hiding the menu. In a later section, I'll transform this information into a CSS media query.

Adding Content for Printer

In some cases, it may be desirable to add content to a page that will only be displayed. For reports, this might be to include criteria used, or perhaps user and a timestamp if not typically included in the print margins.

To explore this scenario, add another classic report region to your page using Listing 20-1. Since there are only three columns, modify the region attributes template to *Value Attribute Pairs - Column*, and hide pagination. Drag the region above the Employees report.

Listing 20-1. SQL Query Returning Data to Be Added When Printing

```
select OWA_UTIL.get_cgi_env ('REQUEST_PROTOCOL') || '://'
    || OWA_UTIL.get_cgi_env ('HTTP_HOST') || ':'
    || OWA_UTIL.get_cgi_env ('SERVER_PORT')
    || OWA_UTIL.get_cgi_env ('SCRIPT_NAME')
    || OWA_UTIL.get_cgi_env ('PATH_INFO') || '?'
    || OWA_UTIL.get_cgi_env ('QUERY_STRING')  url
  ,v('APP_USER') app_user
  ,systimestamp time
from dual
```

Add `print-only` to the CSS classes attribute on the region. By adding a class to such regions, we can hide these using the not operand within a media query, which means you don't need to do anything more to hide this region.

Add Media Queries

Translating the identified IDs and classes into a media query is as simple as defining the CSS as you normally would, and then wrapping the `@media` call around it with some more curly braces. Now add Listing 20-2 to the Inline CSS for the page.

Listing 20-2. CSS to Hide Components from Print Preview

```
/* Hide components from print */
@media print {
  /* selected component types */
  #t_Body_nav /* nav menu */
  ,#apexDevToolbar
  ,.t-Header /* top bar */
  ,.t-Button /* buttons */
  ,.t-Body-topButton
  ,.t-Footer /* footer */
    { display : none !important}
```

```
/* Not only hide menu, but remove margin made for menu */
form .t-Body .t-Body-main {
  margin-left: 0 !important;
  -webkit-transform: none;
  transform: none !important;
}
form .t-Body .t-Body-main>div {
  margin-left: 0 !important;
}

/* remove checkbox column from reoprt */
#p2_emps td[headers=AJAX_CHECKBOX], #p2_emps #AJAX_CHECKBOX
  {display : none;}

}


/* Anything with print-only class
   is only shown when printed */
@media not print {
  .print-only
    { display : none; }
}
```

The second @media query in Listing 20-2 referred to a class that can be added to page components so they are hidden when the device is *not* print media.

Despite trying to avoid the use of the !important attribute, in this case CSS specificity wasn't enough. Results may also vary across browsers, depending on how they honour the CSS. Chrome actually did not remove the menu from the print preview, though it did so while emulating the printer. This was only after refreshing the page as instructed to spoof the user agent, as shown in Figure 20-6.

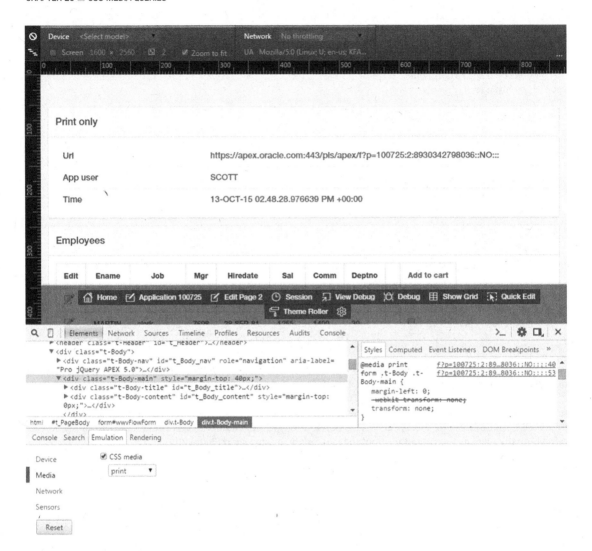

Figure 20-6. *Browser emulating print*

The best test is to print your page. You should note the final layout is cleaner and the extra region is displayed, as per conditions in the supplied CSS.

Hiding Columns by Device Orientation

You will need to start considering orientation as soon as your application is used on a handheld device. Needs will all depend on the application, but you may need to remove non-critical columns from a report when in portrait. Figure 20-7 demonstrates how basic geometry will force assessment of report layouts.

Figure 20-7. *Columns with minimum width can impact portrait mode*

Supplementary regions might also be hidden if they don't adapt to the page and float below the report. One option to conserve space for important information in portrait is to hide non-critical columns. This can also apply when reducing screen width. Listing 20-3 hides the manager and hire date column when either media query is true.

Listing 20-3. Media Query to Hide Column When Portrait or Thin Width

```
/* Hide columns when portrait or thin width screen */
@media (max-width: 800px), (orientation:portrait) {
    #p2_emps td[headers="HIREDATE"], #p2_emps #HIREDATE
    ,#p2_emps td[headers="MGR"], #p2_emps #MGR
       {display: none;}
}
```

Figure 20-8 highlights the hidden columns and shows the media query applied to the hire date column.

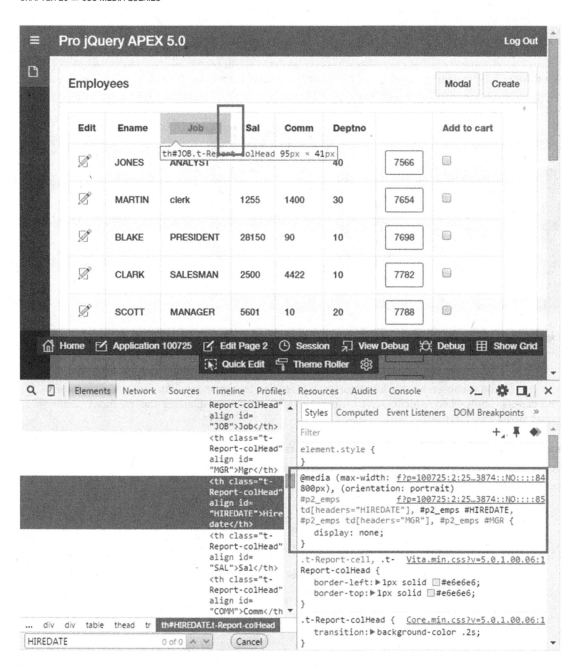

Figure 20-8. *Columns hidden thanks to max-width media query*

Each column is identified by the header and the row cells. Interactive reports may have different selectors.

Summary

On their own, CSS media queries are a useful device for web development, and they will continue to be important as the types of devices rendering web pages becomes more diverse.

This chapter showed how jQuery can interrogate the attributes set by the media conditions, allowing developers to add device-specific logic in their web applications.

Even without jQuery, it's easy to expand standard CSS to construct APEX applications that are more responsive to their environment. Media queries can circumvent the need to open the page in printer-friendly mode before printing, or simply respond to users rotating their device.

CHAPTER 21

■ ■ ■

Coding for the Future

My aim for this book has been to help provide the tools an APEX developer needs to create smarter, more interactive applications using jQuery. I also hope to incite some ideas among the veterans.

I expect most readers to come from an Oracle background looking to learn how to adapt their skills to jQuery. For this reason, I haven't dived too deeply into the jQuery world, in part because I'm still on the journey myself. This book is about integrating jQuery with APEX, not jQuery alone. Starting with essential jQuery fundamentals, and then provided some practical examples with explanations of how APEX page components piece together. All the while covering the important interaction between the browser and the database.

If I had time for more content in the book I would have explored namespaces and instrumentation (debugging), but since there is only so much that can be covered by a writer with a toddler, I would like to conclude with some thoughts to keep in mind as you learn to interact with jQuery. All are patterns I would hope developers apply, even in the language they're most comfortable with, so the topics shouldn't be too unfamiliar. Of course, in this case, it will be with jQuery within APEX in mind.

Embracing Versatility

I use the term "embracing versatility" because jQuery is quite a flexible tool. It can and has been applied to solve a variety of problems and, with basic understanding, you can produce more interactive applications. For APEX developers, this often starts with more flexibility when defining dynamic actions, using jQuery selectors instead of more declarative options. Then the magic of invoking PL/SQL callbacks from JavaScript and everything in between and beyond.

However, there is a balance to be made. Developers must recognize over time not to confuse jQuery as a hammer where your web page is full of nails. You can use jQuery for just about everything, but that doesn't mean you should.

There are questions out there that can be solved with a relatively simple line of jQuery. Recently a question was asked on the OTN forum regarding placeholder text on the interactive report search bar. I could find nothing declarative within APEX, so I used the browser tools to determine the identifier for the field at runtime and then defined this to execute on page load:

```
$('.a-IRR-search-field').attr('placeholder','Hello universe');
```

Simple, effective, but often something that is offered declaratively within APEX. For instance, page items offer the same setting as an attribute under the Appearance section shown in Figure 21-1.

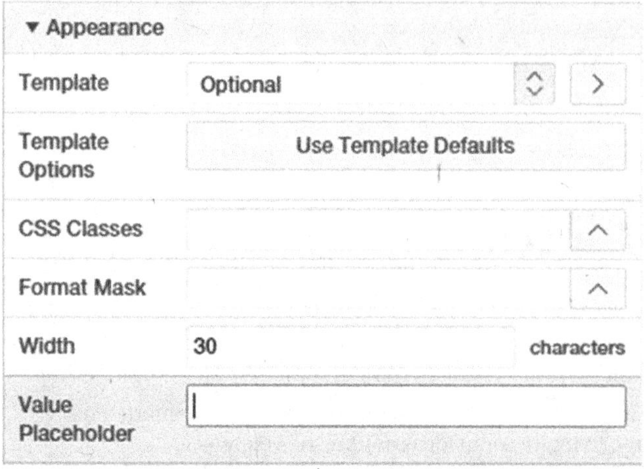

Figure 21-1. Page item declarative attribute that sets ghost text for the item

I always like to think of a mantra I learned from Tom Kyte many years ago: "if it can be done in SQL, do it in SQL." On a web page many things can be done once the page has been rendered, but generating HTML pages with APEX means we have some manner of control and jQuery may not be necessary.

Sometimes the solution is somewhere in between, and this is where APEX has consistently provided generic attributes to provide extra content during page render. Figure 21-2 shows how to provide extra content to page components using Link Attributes, in this case adding classes to a report column link so it will render like a template button.

Figure 21-2. Link Attributes in a link report column

This attribute is available on many types of components. For instance, the button template incorporates this information via the #BUTTON_ATTRIBUTES# substitution string. Unlike other strings such as #JAVASCRIPT# and #BUTTON_ID#, it sits by itself so anything supplied will be rendered verbatim and should be syntactically complete:

```
<button onclick="#JAVASCRIPT#"
  class="t-Button #BUTTON_CSS_CLASSES#"
  type="button"
  #BUTTON_ATTRIBUTES#
  id="#BUTTON_ID#">
<span class="t-Button-label">#LABEL#</span>
</button>
```

Another classic example is font colors in report columns, conditional by row. You could run a jQuery command to test the rows and apply color when true, or you could build the condition into the SQL and incorporate the color within the column HTML expression. The latter means all the work is done by the database as it's determining HTML content, not extra work done by the browser once the page has loaded. The following example is direct from the help for HTML Expression attribute, in this case parameterising classes for a span surrounding the employee status:

```
<span class="#COLUMN_CLASS#">#EMPLOYEE_STATUS#</span>
```

You embrace the versatility of such an adaptable feature by knowing when you don't need to use it. This also goes for APEX. Don't define a PL/SQL action with a NULL; statement in a dynamic action just to use the Page Items to Submit attribute, see Figure 21-3.

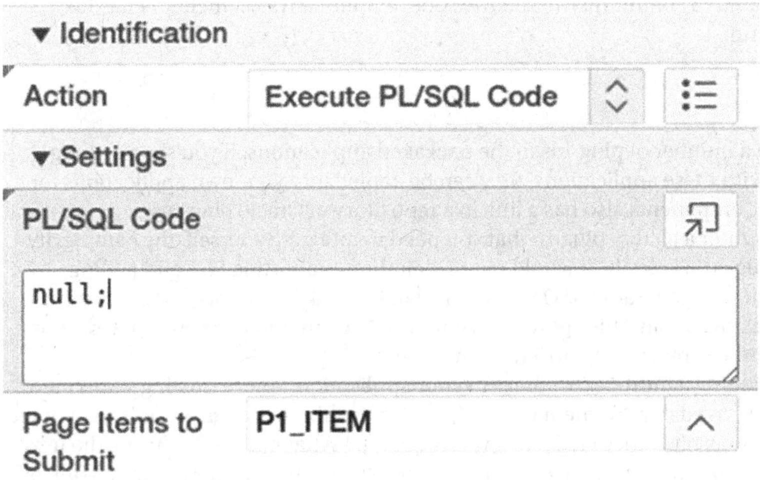

Figure 21-3. *Please avoid doing this*

Instead the same attribute can be found on the report or chart you're refreshing. This saves a round trip to the database, which sounds like something I would have said when programming Oracle Forms.

Don't Reinvent the Wheel

This old adage certainly applies in the world of jQuery. Many problems solved for development projects are done so in a particular pattern, which lends to libraries being built for sharing and re-use. It's so easy to incorporate jQuery frameworks to your application, but don't make the decision to do it lightly.

When looking to solve problems, think about how often that problem may have been encountered before. If you need a function to perform a typical task, chances are there's already a library function available.

Often developers only need to go as far as the supplied APIs, so I highly recommend bookmarking the APEX API Reference defined in the documentation. The APEX 5.0 documentation can be found with the following shortcut, and the best books are linked on the landing page:

```
apex.oracle.com/doc50
```

However, sometimes the Oracle documentation needs supplementation by the jQuery documentation, since methods such as `apex.server.process()` are simply wrappers to jQuery methods:

```
api.jquery.com/jquery.ajax/
```

For larger problems, it could be worth considering incorporating a third-party plug-in. In some cases, you might find an APEX plug-in that bolts all the relevant features to and from the database into the jQuery library. Charting solutions using the D3 framework is a good example. Such plug-ins can be found at a community based repository:

```
apex-plugin.com
```

In October 2015, a site dedicated to community-based APEX development was launched. Plug-ins hosted on GitHub can also be found:

```
apex.world
```

Oracle has also incorporated a number of plug-ins in the packaged applications. If you see anything interesting while experimenting with these applications, they can be copied into your own applications for use. The Plug-ins page in Shared Components also has a link to a repository of Oracle plug-ins.

In other cases, you may encounter a jQuery plug-in that you need to integrate yourself, the complexity of which really depends on the plug-in. Typically, it would entail including supporting files and adding JavaScript into your application, maybe generating JSON from the database, as I described in Chapter 14. This doesn't mean you need to define it as an APEX plug-in as it may only be required for one page in your application, or it may be a menu that is integrated into a List template.

Either way, if you end up including a third-party library in your application, you're trusting someone else's code. Granted, you may have saved development time in utilizing the library, saving a good percentage of total coding effort, but what if it doesn't work exactly how you require it? What if it breaks during the next APEX upgrade? Can you wait for the original authors to supply an update, or can you fix the plug-in yourself?

By all means, incorporate plug-ins to your application. They will save time and help produce a better application, but be prepared to take ownership and treat the code as your own.

Learning Process

Your code will get better over time. Mine certainly does. I've seen it improve during the course of writing this book. I didn't have to modify chapters just because of the APEX 5.0 release. I had to refactor JavaScript my old-fashioned procedural brain wrote.

Consider the PL/SQL you wrote when you first started learning Oracle technology. Remember seeing it again a few years in? It was terrible, or at least ugly. And since there are a number of different ways to solve every jQuery problem, I expect to get critical but constructive feedback on some examples in the book.

Don't expect to be able to conquer the world, but start small and stay close to what you're familiar with. Remember the continual parallels of jQuery to PL/SQL, and the web page to a relational but hierarchical database.

JavaScript has some strange behaviors that are unfamiliar to Oracle developers. Basic syntactic differences can hold basic traps, such as a boolean operator that looks like a PL/SQL concatenator. The following statement will execute successfully but always just return 'value:', seemingly with no value as in JavaScript the double pipe || is really an OR, not a concatenation operand as it is in Oracle:

```
console.log('value:'||this.data);
```

Other JavaScript programming principles will take a little while getting used to, such as equality operators and how JavaScript handles nulls. It's also worth looking into some of the stranger JavaScript behaviors such as hoisting in regard to variable scope.

Debugging

More formally known as instrumentation, logging information about the progress of your code should be inherent to your project code. Without it we wouldn't enjoy tools such as dictionary views and tracing. Tom Kyte specifically addresses instrumentation in a 2005 blog post and frequently talks about it at conferences.

```
http://tkyte.blogspot.com.au/2005/06/instrumentation.html
```

Regarding the use of `console.log()`, realistically your applications will be using the supplied apex. debug namespace, which at the very least means your debug logs will only appear whilst in debug mode.

You could enhance the value of your JavaScript debugging further with the use of a console wrapper created by Martin D'Souza.

```
https://github.com/martindsouza/js-console-wrapper
```

The library behaves in a similar pattern to the PL/SQL precursor called Logger, which you should also utilize in your PL/SQL. The JavaScript wrapper allows basic calls such as this one to automatically output all parameters sent to a function.

```
$.console.logParams();
```

The PL/SQL version of the library is available at the OraOpenSource project site.

```
http://www.oraopensource.com/logger/
```

Processes

Callback behavior will often trap newcomers to the language, particularly in our case as we're often invoking PL/SQL asynchronously from JavaScript. This means statements subsequent to the server process will execute before the process returns:

```
apex.server.process
  ("CB_HELLO"
  ,{pageItems : '#P1_EMPNO'}
).done(function() {
  console.log('I will run second');
});
console.log('I will run first');
```

Some of the biggest traps in AJAX processing relate to how information is interchanged between the browser and session state in the database, often using those Page Items to Submit/Return attributes.

Once you understand session state, the next hurdle becomes the asynchronous nature of these processes in the web world. Read through chapters 9 and 14 carefully. Familiarize yourself well with regard to how the .done() method delegates action upon return from PL/SQL, and the use of .then() to formulate dependency chains.

Behavior regarding the Wait for Result attribute in PL/SQL events for dynamic actions will likely change in APEX 5.1 as the team prepares to remove the use of the deprecated async parameter, so stay tuned for information from Oracle.

Namespaces

I recommend learning to use namespaces in JavaScript. It's a tough topic as there are many different ways to code them, but they basically allow you to organize your code into logical blocks of functionality just like you do with packages in the database.

I used this to encapsulate code from one page in chapter 14. This can be simplified to the following code that wraps methods foo and bar within a named space:

```
var myApp_p2 = {

  foo: function() {
  }

  ,bar: function() {
  }
};
```

Individual functions can then be referred to using the following:

```
myApp_p2.foo();
```

JavaScript functions do not have the same checks and balances that stored PL/SQL procedures face in the database to validate their definition, so namespaces can be vital in avoiding collisions with other objects and variables in the global namespace, particularly with larger projects. Start doing this from the beginning, because some projects tend to grow quickly.

Finally, in regard to your learning process, pay attention to the JavaScript frameworks that are delivering successes in the community. For instance, Node.js now provides APEX developers vast array of functionality along with strong community support from sites such as

jsao.io

Performance

I'm often thinking about performance when I write SQL and PL/SQL, particularly now with its integration with the Internet of Things through technologies like Oracle APEX. jQuery also has performance aspects in regard to how it locates page components and modifies the DOM.

The analogy to Oracle can still apply with respect to indexing and context switching. As Oracle technologists, we can be aware of a few things to cover the most important aspects of jQuery performance, and you may recall some of these concepts from Chapter 2.

Selectors

You need to ensure the selectors used are done so to minimize the work required by the browser to find your DOM objects. Identifying components the right way with IDs, classes, and tags can make a difference when traversing the DOM, much like querying a table with a selective index can make a query execute faster.

A few basic patterns can help you stay on course. In fact, applying a static ID to a region as per Figure 21-4 so you can isolate your logic to a particular region is exactly what you need to comply with some basic jQuery best practices.

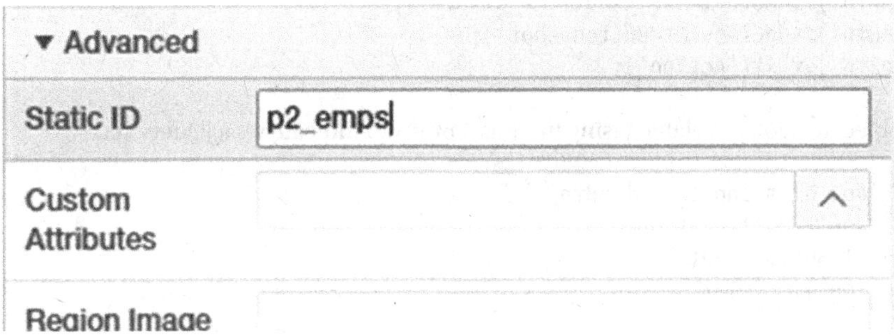

Figure 21-4. Setting region static ID

The fastest selector in jQuery is the ID selector, so identifying the region using $('#p2_emps') is fast as it maps directly to a native JavaScript method, getElementById().

Selecting multiple elements using classes is a useful utility, such as a jQuery selector for a dynamic action listing for clicks on buttons in the report. However, selecting using just the class is slow, so to minimize the performance hit always descent from the closest parent ID. In this case, the region makes a convenient parent, saving jQuery from traversing the entire DOM:

$('#p2_emps .actionBtn')

This could be improved further by prefixing the class with the relevant tag:

```
$('#p2_emps input.actionBtn')
```

Don't bother prefixing an ID with a tag name such as div#p2_emps as this can be likened to prefixing a % in your SQL, such as WHERE indexed_column LIKE '%WESLEY'. The Oracle example will ignore the index, whereas in jQuery it will locate all <div> elements on the page looking for the ID.

From a performance perspective, it's redundant to include multiple IDs. However, it may be logically accurate, such as identifying columns within a report region:

```
$('#p2_emps #ENAME')
```

The take away is to always prefix a class with a tag name, and remember to descend from an ID.

Caching

When I worked in Oracle Forms, I used to cache the pointer to certain items that were used all the time using the following:

```
item_id ITEM := FIND_ITEM('EMP.ENAME');
```

This way every time I needed to be interactive with that item, I could do so in the fastest way possible, similar to having the rowid of a record in a table. The same can be done in jQuery by caching jQuery objects to a variable. The following code locates the jQuery objects three times to apply three different methods:

```
$('#p2_emps input.actionBtn').removeClass('t-Button--simple');
$('#p2_emps input.actionBtn').addClass('t-Button--hot');
$('#p2_emps input.actionBtn').text('Action');
```

Instead, first save the object to a local variable, using the $ as a prefix to indicate it's a jQuery set.

```
var $report_buttons = $('#p2_emps input.actionBtn')
$report_buttons.removeClass('t-Button--simple');
$report_buttons.addClass('t-Button--hot');
$report_buttons.text('Action');
```

In reality, these references might be scattered around the page in different dynamic actions. The idea here is to never repeat a jQuery selection operation. You can even write subqueries using these saved objects:

```
$report_buttons.find('span')
```

Chaining

A common technique to apply a number of methods to a jQuery selector is to chain the commands. If required in one command, the previous example could be re-written in the following way:

```
$('#p2_emps input.actionBtn')
  .removeClass('t-Button--simple');
  .addClass('t-Button--hot');
  .text('Action');
```

It saves the browser extra work in finding the element each time, essentially removing the context switching between JavaScript and interrogating the DOM, just like minimizing context switching in PL/SQL using bulk binding.

The same context switching argument is made when manipulating the DOM. More advanced JavaScript code may loop through to build HTML content. Instead of modifying the DOM within the loop, you should build the string and then modify the DOM after the loop is complete.

Event Delegation

Event delegation is the technical term for an example I first mentioned in Chapter 6 in regard to defining a click event in a report. You could start the on Click definition by selecting the buttons within a region:

```
$('#p2_emps input.actionBtn').on('click', function() { ...
```

Or you could set the event at the parent level and determine what was clicked within the region. jQuery offers a selector parameter to filter descendants of the selected elements that will call the handler, much like the WHEN clause in an Oracle table trigger can filter only modifications to a certain column:

```
$('#p2_emps').on('click', 'input.actionBtn', function() { ...
```

Not only is this more efficient, but the event is still relevant should the region be refreshed. The first method would need to be reapplied after refresh of the region as the event is on the individual elements. This concept relates to the Static/Dynamic Event Scope options in dynamic actions.

Build Content into the Render

The code executed in the hypothetical report button may need to make logic decisions on data not visible in the report. As I described in Chapter 8, one method is to include this information as custom attributes on the button. The HTML Expression or Link Attributes could include a custom data-* attribute:

```
data-mystatus="#MY_STATUS#"
```

Then the JavaScript event can read this information using the following:

```
$(this.triggeringElement).data('mystatus')
```

This saves another trip to the database when a click occurs, though be aware the data in the report may be stale. This means another user may have updated it, so you should remember the optimistic nature of APEX and respond to any final DML failure.

Performance Testing

I suspect most of the jQuery APEX developers use do not need strenuous performance testing, but you can load test variations of solutions to jQuery snippets at the following site:

`jsperf.com`

Modularization

I also count maintenance as performance cost. You should already be modularizing and encapsulating PL/SQL within packages in the database. The same rings true for jQuery. A good portion of your jQuery should probably live in .js files either in the APEX repository or on your web file server. This could be done at page, user interface, theme, and/or project level depending on the intent of the jQuery.

Combined with the use of namespaces, your experience with jQuery libraries can be very similar to the dot notation used in Oracle.

Resources

The Internet is a big place, so it goes without saying that there are multiple avenues available when looking for resources online. For me, this information comes in three major avenues.

References

There are a number of documentation pages I bookmark and visit regularly as a quick lookup for syntax and behaviors—one can't remember everything. The beauty of many of these pages is the information you need is at most one click away:

- SQL Reference (12c): Oracle manual that provides quick link to all single row functions and DDL

  `https://docs.oracle.com/database/121/SQLRF/toc.htm`

- APEX API Reference: Common libraries available to all developers

  `apex.oracle.com/doc50`

- jQuery Selectors: Quick reference sheet

  `http://www.w3schools.com/jquery/jquery_ref_selectors.asp`

- jQuery Cheat Sheet: Quick link to formal documentation for common jQuery methods, grouped by category

  `http://oscarotero.com/jquery/`

- Cross Browser Compatibility: For those occasions where you need to ensure the attributes you use are available across all browsers you need to support

  `http://caniuse.com/`

- JSON Parser: to help test the format

  `http://json.parser.online.fr/`

- Color Hexa: best site I've found to help make sensible color decisions

  `http://www.colorhexa.com/`

- Icons: lookups for Font Awesome and jQuery icons respectively

  `http://fortawesome.github.io/Font-Awesome/icons/`

  `http://roam.be/lab/jquery-ui-icon-name-map/`

Note that when searching for HTML and CSS attributes, some people prefer the detail that Mozilla Developer Network (MDN) provides over the lightweight W3Schools.

Assistance

Of course, there are times when documentation is not enough and we need assistance from others. If you do not have colleagues with whom to talk problems through, I find two particular forums helpful depending on the technology.

The OTN forums hosted by Oracle are the idea place for any Oracle-related question. A dedicated space is available for APEX, and other spaces available for related technologies like ORDS, SQL Developer, SQL, and PL/SQL:

`community.oracle.com`

jQuery questions related to APEX are also posed and answered here, but the jQuery specific questions are best resolved at `stackoverflow.com`.

You'll find many frequent questions have already been asked and the forum ensures the best responses are emphasized, with pertinent comments nearby.

Twitter is also a tool I've used to ask for community comment, and you can find many of the Oracle ACEs in this platform. An environment for more targeted community discussion can be found at the Oracle APEX channel at Slack:

`orclapex.slack.com`

For those who do not want to register at these sites, you can information aggregated at `apex.world`.

There are plenty of developers out there willing to volunteer assistance, though I encourage you to learn how to ask questions effectively and provide test cases where possible.

New Information

As an APEX developer, I can safely say it will be a long time before we stop learning and there's only so much we can do ourselves through experimentation. A number of APEX developers blog regularly about various aspects of the tool, and many posts do relate to the progress of web technologies and how to apply them. These posts are aggregated at `odtug.com/apex`.

You could use an RSS reader such as Feedly to organize your own selection of feeds and read them at your leisure. Please add a positive comment when you find a blog post useful—such gratitude goes a long way.

Also stay in touch with what developers around the world are accomplishing by hearing what they have to say. This learning opportunity also applies to presentations at conferences that are often available to either stream or download the related slides.

Summary

Oracle APEX is a flexible development tool further enhanced by jQuery, the browser's language. Like many languages, if you find parallels to those you're comfortable with, you'll find them easier to learn.

I enjoy developing so much I have a passion for it. With geographic isolation, I need to find other ways of sharing my experiences and I hope my enthusiasm comes across in this book. Now it's up to you to learn from the examples and then adapt and apply them to your niche set of problems.

Anyone who stops learning is old, whether at twenty or eighty. Anyone who keeps learning stays young. The greatest thing in life is to keep your mind young. —Henry Ford

Erratum to: Pro jQuery in Oracle Application Express

Scott Wesley

Erratum to:
Chapter 9 in: Scott Wesley, *Pro jQuery in Oracle Application Express*,
DOI 10.1007/978-1-4842-0961-5_9

Chapter 9 was inadvertently published without the incorporation of the final corrections it is now updated with the corrections both in the chapter and front matter.

The updated original online version for this chapter can be found at
DOI 10.1007/978-1-4842-0961-5_9

Scott Wesley
39 Watkins Loop, Tapping WA 6065
Australia
e-mail: wesleyscott79@gmail.com

Index

 *For the Complete Technology & Database Professional*

IOUG represents the **voice of Oracle technology and database professionals -** empowering you to be **more productive in your business** and career by **delivering education,** sharing **best practices** and providing technology direction and **networking opportunities.**

Context, Not Just Content

IOUG is dedicated to helping our members become an #IOUGenius by staying on the cutting-edge of Oracle technologies and industry issues through practical content, user-focused education, and invaluable networking and leadership opportunities:

- *SELECT Journal* is our quarterly publication that provides in-depth, peer-reviewed articles on industry news and best practices in Oracle technology

- Our #IOUGenius blog highlights a featured weekly topic and provides **content driven by Oracle professionals and the IOUG community**

- Special Interest Groups provide you the chance to collaborate with peers on the specific issues that matter to you and even take on leadership roles outside of your organization

- COLLABORATE is our once-a-year opportunity to connect with the members of not one, but three, Oracle users groups (IOUG, OAUG and Quest) as well as with the top names and faces in the Oracle community.

Who we are...

... **more than 20,000** database professionals, developers, application and infrastructure architects, business intelligence specialists and IT managers

... **a community of users** that share experiences and knowledge on issues and technologies that matter to you and your organization

Interested? Join IOUG's community of Oracle technology and database professionals at **www.ioug.org/Join.**

Independent Oracle Users Group | phone: (312) 245-1579 | email: membership@ioug.org
330 N. Wabash Ave., Suite 2000, Chicago, IL 60611

Printed in the United States
By Bookmasters